"Alexandra Kennedy has provided a beautiful and deeply personal demonstration of how shamanic training can help one survive the tragedies and challenges of life."
— Michael Harner, author of *The Way of the Shaman*

"Alexandra Kennedy has written a wonderful book that provides a deep and moving account of her experiences in dealing with her father's death. She eloquently explains her own grieving and how she used the grieving process in her own psychological and spiritual journey. This is truly a pioneering look at the spiritual dimensions of loss and grieving."
— Robert Frager, founder and first president of the Institute of Transpersonal Psychology

"This book is going to be tremendously helpful to a lot of people. I think it is one of the best documentations I've seen of the interweavings of inner and outer worlds."
— Hal Zina Bennett, co-author of *Follow Your Bliss*

"A gifted psychotherapist, the author provides practical guidance with potential for unlimited spiritual growth."
— Frances Horn, author of *I Want One Thing*

Losing a Parent

Losing a Parent

Passage to a New Way of Living

Alexandra Kennedy

HarperSanFrancisco

A Division of HarperCollins*Publishers*

To share responses to *Losing a Parent* or to obtain
information regarding workshops and lectures,
you may write:

Alexandra Kennedy
P.O. Box 1866
Soquel, CA 95073

Lines from *Open Secret: Versions of Rumi* by John Moyne and Coleman
Barks, copyright 1984 by Threshold Books (RD 4 Box 600, Putney, Vermont 05346). Used by permission of the publisher.

Excerpt from "East Coker" in *Four Quartets,* copyright 1943 by T. S. Eliot
and renewed by Esme Valerie Eliot, reprinted by permission of Harcourt
Brace Jovanovich, Inc. and Faber and Faber Ltd.

FIRST EDITION

Library of Congress Cataloging-in-Publication Data
Kennedy, Alexandra.
    Losing a parent: passage to a new way of living/Alexandra
Kennedy.—1st ed.
        p.   cm.
    Includes bibliographical references and index.
    ISBN 0–06–250498–3 (alk. paper)
    1. Bereavement—Psychological aspects.   2. Parents—Death—
Psychological aspects.   3. Shamanism—Psychological aspects.
I. Title
BF575.G7K46   1991
155.9'37—dc20
                                                            90–55786
                                                            CIP

99 00 01 HAD 16 15 14

To my mother and father
with love

Contents

Acknowledgments

Six months after my father's death, I began writing for my own healing about the events, both inner and outer, of his dying. However, it was my clients and friends, seeking new perspectives on their own grief, who encouraged me to continue writing for a larger audience. Although I cannot name them here, I want to express my deep gratitude to my clients. Their struggles, stories, questions, challenges, triumphs, and insights have inspired many of the pages of this book. To honor the confidentiality of those whose stories appear in this book, I have changed their names and other identifying details. And I extend heartfelt thanks to my dear friends who supported me emotionally through seemingly endless drafts, sustaining me through the periods of discouragement and sharing in the joys, especially Lois Robin, Jill Hoffman, Eileen Slattery, Kathleen Roberts, Richard Salzburg, David and Gina Hess, Gertrude Karnow, Mackie Ramsay, Ed Demere, Anina and Derek Van Alstine, Isabelle Roselund, Susan and Phil Wagner, and Marsha Newman.

Many colleagues and friends also gave generously of their time and editorial skills, offering invaluable suggestions, especially Barbara Vogl, Michael Warren, and Frances Horn. Special appreciation goes to editor extraordinaire Hal Zina Bennett, who gave this book his support from the earliest stages, his belief in its value motivating me to keep working. I am grateful to Kathleen Roberts for her logo designs of the ancient symbol of the vescia piscis, two interlinking circles that represent the meeting of the visible and invisible worlds. And my thanks to the Capitola Book Cafe for providing an environment so conducive to writing and a hot pot of chai brewing.

My profound gratitude to my editor at HarperSanFrancisco, Michael Toms, for taking such a personal interest in my book and supporting it through its birth pains. I must also express my appreciation to the staff at HarperSanFrancisco for being so skillful in their work and respectful of mine. And special thanks to Mimi Kusch and Mark Salzwedel for their support and encouragement.

Throughout the past two years, a small group of friends has gathered regularly in my living room, committed to exploring the inner realms together. Many of the journeys in this book were experienced and first shared there. These meetings have been for me a continual source of renewal, surprise, and inspiration. I also owe much gratitude to the members of the monthly dream group whose insights over the past seven years have been invaluable to my personal and professional growth.

I want to acknowledge those whose teachings have had a significant impact on my life and hence on this book: Stephen Levine, Michael Harner, Arny Mindell, James Hillman, Ken Ring, and many others named and unnamed in this book. I deeply appreciate two wise people who knew what seeds were germinating unseen within me over the past twenty years and prepared me for their emergence: Lew Fein and Jack Schwarz.

The appearance in my life five years ago of heartful friend and brilliant mentor Ken Ring marked a new chapter. He validated for me the often unusual and sometimes frightening experiences that are so much a part of explorations into inner space, giving them a new context in the light of his own work and research. I thank him for the inspiration of his vision, for his faith in me, and for his encouragement, which have all been such major catalysts to this book that I can in no way adequately acknowledge his contribution.

I am grateful for the love of my family and friends, which has helped make the many months of grieving one of the richest times of my life. To my mother and good friend, with whom I have shared so many passages, I hold out the blossoming rose of our relationship. My thanks to her for instilling in me a love of books and creative expression, but mostly for her ever-present confidence in me. I am just now beginning to acknowledge the full impact of all that my father gave me in life—and in death—rich gifts, indeed, that will take a lifetime to fully integrate. I feel grateful for all the healing that has taken place since his death, opening my heart and our relationship to new depths of acceptance and love. And I thank my son, Taylor, whose expansive spirit, humor, and fresh perspective have shone on my life since his birth, for challenging me to move beyond my own fears and limitations and reach for my dreams—this book being one.

And finally, but most significantly, my love and appreciation go to my husband and best friend, Jon. There are no words to convey how deeply and heartfully he has influenced my life and work—and now this book. Every page reflects his tender and sensitive support through the many phases of my grief, his astute editorial advice, and his ever-deepening love.

Foreword

Most people will have to deal with the death of a parent; few people are at all prepared to.

Alexandra Kennedy wasn't. Despite her years of work as a psychotherapist and her training in meditation, the news of her father's cancer shattered her armor like a lance and left her in anguished shock. Still, the word of her father's impending death wasn't a total surprise; she realized that during the previous year she already had had powerful intimations of it. Nevertheless, the flood of feelings and terrible pain that poured out from the wound opened by her father's terminal illness astonished and dismayed her.

These feelings also initiated the journey that led to the book you now hold in your hands.

My studies of the near-death experience have shown me that a close brush with death can, despite its trauma, launch the survivor on a journey that radically transforms his or her life— and his or her view of death. Through the implacable face of her father's impending death, Alexandra discovered another, and much more common, pathway to this kind of personal realization. For the prospect of *another's* death may also trigger a process that leads one out of the complacent routines of one's life and into the deep recesses of the psyche where the healing journey always must begin.

In Alexandra's case, it led in a relatively short time to her discovery of an inner world of intensely real images that somehow mirrored and gave heightened meaning to the events in the outward world concerning her father and her changing relationship to him. In fact, with the help of a distinguished explorer of this realm, Michael Harner, she had found her way into what is traditionally called "the shamanic world."

A shaman is usually conceived to be an intermediary between the world of ordinary sensory experience and the supersensory world. And a shaman's art, which is essentially that of healing, is based on the shaman's ability to draw information from his or her sojourns in the invisible world and bring it to bear on our familiar world of time and space. In her own journeys, Alexandra soon discerned what is obvious to practitioners of shamanism throughout the world but so difficult for us modern Westerners to believe: this inner world is fully *real* in its own terms, with a coherent geography and recurrently appearing animals and personal guides. Once one learns—and she learned quickly—to cultivate the imaginal faculties that give one access to this world, one can consciously enter into this domain beyond the senses and be taught directly by powers of one's own psyche. Retaining these insights—which are vividly implanted into one's awareness through incredibly searing hyperreal experiences—and applying them to one's everyday life allows one to bridge the worlds.

No one should suppose, however, that doing so is merely a matter of cultivating one's inherent power of imagery. That is only the perceptual requirement. Fundamental to the true shamanic quest is some kind of death-and-rebirth process in which the everyday self is wrenched from its secure moorings and made to hazard the turbulent night sea without a compass and without any guarantee of eventual safe landing. The descriptions of Alexandra's own journeys into the shamanic realm, though often full of radiantly beautiful and vivid images, offer ample evidence of how harrowing and testing these ordeals can be.

The undeniable rewards of such experiences, nevertheless, are soon evident as Alexandra finds a strange symbolic counterpoint developing between what she experiences in her inner journeys and the events leading to her father's death. Her grief over the approaching loss of her father, her memories of her emotionally truncated but still loving relationship with him, her frustrations over his refusal to confront his illness openly, and even the stages of his illness and eventual death—all these are illuminated with such subtle and deeply meaningful shafts of insight through her imaginal journeys that one feels she has thereby gained direct access to her own soul's higher wisdom. In this way, she comes to understand and accept her father's death and begins to see him—and herself—in a new and healing light. And even after he dies, through further imaginal explorations, this healing continues and eventually is completed, not just for Alexandra but, as she makes clear, for her father also. As she states, "death ends a life, not a relationship," and what remains incomplete at a parent's death may in fact be resolved in the shared imaginal field that can be sustained for a time after that death.

The story of this healing, the means by which it was attained, and the accounts of Alexandra's inner journeys make gripping and edifying reading. But the author is not concerned merely to narrate the personal experiences stimulated by her father's death. Though these certainly give the book its emotional force, their ultimate purpose is really to make us mindful of how woefully ill-prepared most of us are to confront the death of a parent, or even to deal with it years afterward.

Therefore, drawing on her own explorations in shamanic space, her therapy with clients who have unresolved issues around the death of a parent, and her workshops, Alexandra offers readers an array of suggestions and techniques that will enable them to deal effectively with the grief a parent's death causes and to use it as a means of inaugurating their own trans-formative healing journeys.

This, then, is a book that both inspires through the example of the author and teaches us new ways to cope with the wounds that any death will cause. In writing it, Alexandra Kennedy has made us aware that the parent who has given us life may in dying cause us to die—into greater life.

It is Alexandra's gift to show us how to enter it.

Kenneth Ring

Losing a Parent

CHAPTER 1

A Journey Through Grief

The death of a parent is one of the most significant events of our lives. Whether your parent is dying, or has died recently or many years ago, you may be struggling to go on with your life while knowing deep down that something momentous has happened. You may feel buffeted by unbearably intense feelings—anger, sadness, loneliness, despondency, even joy. You may feel numb, curiously unaffected by the death of your parent. Chances are that you have tried hard to put this event behind you too quickly, without tapping its transformative and healing potential.

Or you may feel a need to begin preparing for the loss of your parents, even when they are healthy. You may have been watching your parents grow old for some time, their bodies slowly or rapidly disintegrating, a glaring reminder of their mortality. Too often we avoid even thinking about the death of our parents, leaving the dread to fester inside. If we do not die first, someday we will be forced to confront their deaths and we may not be prepared. It is liberating to confront our denial and accept that our parents will die—perhaps within the next few years or even months. Then we can see the wisdom of learning effective strategies for grieving now. Then we realize that we need to tend to the unfinished business with our parents now, to say to them what we have held back—before it is too late.

As you hold this book, you may feel resistance welling up and think, "I don't have time . . . this would be too overwhelming . . . if I let myself grieve, my life would fall apart . . . something like this would interfere with my other commitments . . . I'm not feeling anything now, so why not leave well enough alone . . . time will take care of everything." This resistance is natural; you are bound to feel it in the face of such powerful forces. Many clients and participants at workshops have expressed their fear that they will be overwhelmed by their grief and left unable to cope in other areas of their lives. Some were concerned that once they started crying they would not be able to stop. Some feared they would go crazy. These same people were relieved to discover the benefits of devoting short periods of time to grieving every day, finding a rhythm of grieving and attending to daily tasks. This approach provides an opportunity to explore the many dimensions of grief without having to abandon your daily responsibilities and commitments.

Even in the face of your resistance, deep down you probably recognize that the loss of your parent has made an indelible mark on your life. This event has changed you; you will never be the same.

The death of a parent is a shattering experience, wounding us and flooding us with powerful forces. The boundaries of our world are torn away, and suddenly life seems bigger than we might ever have imagined, terrifyingly bigger. A parent's death can shatter us, leaving lifetime scars, or it can shatter our limited sense of ourselves, opening up our world into new dimensions. For the latter to happen we must be willing to take a journey through our grief, following what may often seem like a long, dark passage that will, in its own time, open out into vast new worlds.

In the following pages I have shared the struggles, frustrations, woundings, healings, and discoveries of my own journey through grief. Many parts of my story will resonate with your own experience; other parts may seem foreign. At times you may feel inspired or comforted, at other times disturbed or shocked. My story is not intended to be a typical one but is offered as an illustration of the potential for healing and transformation inherent in grief.

After each chapter of my story, you will find exercises and suggestions that can help you explore the healing possibilities through your own passage and prepare you for the momentous discoveries that await you as you emerge into a greater life on the other side.

There is a progression to the exercises, so you may want to familiarize yourself with one section before moving on to the next. Take your time; you may spend days or weeks on one section, exploring the exercises over and over, deepening the experience. Other sections may seem less relevant to your particular needs at this time; you can return to these later. Remember that your experience of grief is unique, even though it may have certain universal features. Feel free to improvise, change, or modify any of the exercises as you feel inspired. Don't hold on to one approach; be willing to let it go when it has served its purpose of healing. Grief is a process of letting go—not just of a loved one but also of concepts, ways of doing things, and experiences.

This, then, is your own journey. You will be provided with a map that delineates the territory to be explored, provisions to sustain you, and basic guidelines to make the passage easier. However, the journey will be a unique experience for each of you; there is so much territory to explore, much of it uncharted. Even well-traveled trails yield new sights and perspectives through different eyes. As on any journey, some of you will hesitate to begin, others will plunge in, some will move slowly and carefully step by step, and others will rush ahead. There will be places of easy passage as well as the inevitable difficulties. Some of you will turn back after the first testings; others will choose to continue on. To all of you, however you make the journey, I wish you healing along the way—a healing into life, and perhaps into a greater life than you ever could have imagined.

CHAPTER 2

The Bubble Bursts

Over the answering machine came the shaken voice of my mother: "Dad has cancer all through his bones. We just heard from the doctor. Don't call me back, because Dad doesn't want anyone to know."

I began to cry in deep sobs as the words sank into my heart. Dad had complained of pain in his hips, which we had thought was arthritis. Surely this was a mistake, a bad dream.

I suddenly felt flooded by undefined, powerful forces that tore through the boundaries of my world, leaving me unprotected. I felt stripped of my skin, left raw and bleeding.

As I sat down, a kaleidoscope of jumbled images, feelings, and memories ran through my body and mind, then shifted into focus, revealing a clear picture. At that moment I knew that Dad would soon die. I realized with a start that on some level I had known this for over a year. My time with him was drawing to a close.

In a dream nine months earlier, Dad had appeared at my hotel room door, holding a white chrysanthemum. I had awakened, shaken by the dream without understanding why. I realized now that he had stood there quietly holding a funeral flower.

In the past year, I had made repeated attempts to connect with him, writing letters and calling him, asking for some time in which we could just be together. I had felt a strange urgency. Not even suspecting that he might be ill, I had sent him a poem I had heard in a 1976 lecture of Elisabeth Kübler-Ross, a psychiatrist

4

who has dedicated her life to teaching new attitudes toward death and dying. This poem was written by a man after his father's death:

> When you love give it everything you've got and when you've reached your limit give it more. And forget the pain of it because if you face your death it is only the love you have given and received which will count and all the rest—the accomplishments, the struggles, the fights—will be forgotten in your reflection.
>
> And if you have loved well then it will have been worth it and the thrill of it will last you through the end. And if you have not, death will always come too soon and be too terrible to face.

I had taken a risk in sending this, since my father avoided talking about death. I remember one vivid example. My son, Taylor, a curious six-year-old, was filled with questions about death when his cat died. One night he looked at his granddad and asked, "Are you going to die, Granddad?" My father gruffly dismissed the question with a short "Of course not."

Now I was struck by the realization that part of me had known the future long before I was consciously aware of it. That part had prodded me to send the letters and the Kübler-Ross passage. A month previously I had written in my journal:

> This then is my journey, the unfolding of my life to the present time. It will continue to unfold, surprising me all along the way. Even though unexpected things keep happening to me, there seems to be an underlying flow, as though everything were developing naturally.
>
> New changes are already stirring within me, a now-familiar pressure, restlessness, and chaos that will in its own time give birth to something new. Now-familiar outer signs confirm this inner sense—my dreams have yielded many initiation themes and I've caught myself humming "Something's Coming" from *West Side Story*. A 260-foot well was just completed on our land yielding seventy gallons a minute—

perhaps if I am willing to go deep enough within myself I will come upon a bounty of resources beyond my wildest expectations.

While the magnitude of the change that I sense around the corner frightens me at times, I welcome and trust the infinite and ungraspable workings of the invisible thread as it weaves through my life.

Although part of me fought admitting it, wanting my father to live into old age, I recognized that on some level he was choosing to die in the prime of his life, with his full powers still intact. There was nothing about old age that he looked forward to. Dreaded retirement was now looming right over his shoulder, perhaps even months away. He was terrified of growing old. He couldn't bear illness and fought giving in to colds and flus. I rarely saw him stay in bed, no matter how sick he felt.

In completely characteristic manner, he insisted on going on with his life as usual. Perhaps he hoped that what he ignored would just go away. His cancer was his secret, known only to my mother and his doctor. I was now in on the secret, but for a time we had to play a game of my not knowing. That tore me apart inside. As the days passed I felt caught in a nightmare, unable to talk to my father about the cancer, feeling weighed down by sorrow and anger. I resented my role of quiet support, a role I had accepted since childhood.

I was suddenly aware that I couldn't play by these rules with my parents any longer—but I could see no way out. Though my father and mother chose not to talk about the cancer and their fears, I knew that I had to acknowledge my own fears. I shared my tears, fears, and frustrations with my husband, Jon. I began talking to my close friends too, feeling guilty that I was betraying my father's secret.

By Thanksgiving, Dad became aware that I knew about his cancer. I sat on the couch in my parents' living room, holding his warm hand and talking about light subjects that felt very disconnected to anything either of us were feeling. As I looked at him, it was hard to accept that cancer was embedded deep in his strong, vital body. I looked for signs. His thick, gray hair framed a ruddy face—he had no thinning hair or pale, drawn complexion. His brown eyes flickered brightly from under a wiry tangle of eyebrows as he talked and then faded during our silences; perhaps then he retreated into thoughts of his illness. His large, muscular body promised compact power and delivered a large, resonating voice. I could perceive no weakening there.

Dad was an imposing man, large in spirit and in body. A room vibrated with his presence when he entered it. He gravitated to people, clasping their hands, touching their shoulders, giving a compliment, sharing a story in his gruff though warm manner. He knew how to make people feel good about themselves. He knew how to make people feel special. This was his art, his gift.

To many of his friends he seemed invincible to the ravages of time, an image he sought to perpetuate. At seventy-three, he was still rising at 5:30 A.M., working in two top management positions, and flying all over the world on business trips. And now the myth was challenged: he was human, vulnerable. I noticed when he shifted his body on the couch that he was hurting; this was the first sign he let me see of any illness.

He squeezed my hand gently, perhaps to comfort me, and a powerful current of love flowed through our hands, as it always had. I felt a great sadness that we had been so distant with so much love flowing beneath. I wanted in those moments to break down with him and cry, share with him my grief, my fear of losing him, my yearning to bridge that intangible space that separated us. Stephen Levine, one of my first meditation teachers, often pointed out in his retreats that grief uncovers the separateness we've always felt with loved ones.

During my early years while my father was away at war, the many months of physical separation had disrupted our early bonding. Our relationship was always to alternate between short periods of strong connection and long periods of emotional distance. Ever so briefly I would be treated, as I was on the couch that day, to the expression of his love flowing through his warm hand as it wrapped around mine. I loved his hands, for they shared spontaneously the sensitivity that he had managed to conceal with his often gruff demeanor.

Throughout my childhood I had accompanied him to church. Sitting on the wooden pew next to him, I had felt peaceful, curiously watching his absorbed face as he prayed. He often held my hand then, too. My hand still is imprinted with the memory of his reassuring touch.

Then suddenly the walls would go up again; he had retreated into his shell. As I grew up, I had a hard time reconciling the father who was very warm and expressive with the father who was extremely private and awkward in intimate situations.

At the Thanksgiving meal, Dad sat straight, revealing no sign of the physical pain I knew he was feeling. Mother had worked hard to prepare a delicious dinner, with the creamed onions and gravy that he loved. She knew that this well might be his last Thanksgiving. As the five of us—Mother, Father, my husband, Jon, my son, Taylor, and I—gathered around the table, we waited for the traditional words of grace. Dad bowed his head, closed his eyes, and said a prayer, ending with the words, "Lord, we pray for the love, strength, and courage we all may need in the coming months." Jon and I glanced across the table with tears brimming.

The weeks passed, Dad maintaining his regular demanding executive schedule. When he came home at night, he collapsed in pain. By the middle of December, the doctor announced that the cancer had spread to the liver, and that his bones were already breaking from the disease. The doctors still could not find the source of the cancer, but they felt that it had to be the prostate, even though a biopsy was negative. Dad was initiated into the hospital routine during those tests; it was only the second hospitalization of his life, the first having been for minor surgery. Immediately following the tests he was discharged, only to return again with a high fever from an infection contracted during the tests.

I visited him at the hospital. He looked so lonely lying in the barren, green-walled room, surrounded by IVs. When the doctor appeared on his rounds, Dad, usually the one in command of a situation, looked up at him and asked very quietly, "Are we going to lick this, doctor?" That moment is forever imprinted in my memory. I wanted to bend down and hold my father, for I had never seen him look so vulnerable. The doctor, clearly put on the spot, smiled and said, "We'll do our best." The attempt at a cheery attitude could not dispel the gravity that hung thick in the air.

When Dad emerged from the hospital a week later, he again went on with business as usual. The doctor applauded this attitude, insisting that it would be harmful to tell my father how serious his illness was when he seemed so optimistic. Mother bore the burden of the prognosis, keeping it a secret from Dad that he had only a few months to a year to live, and she turned to me with each new crisis. I passed the days with my stomach in a perpetual state of turbulence and my chest raw, a great sadness and helplessness weighing on me. I dreaded the ring of the telephone, since nearly every day it brought me news of another critical development. I had barely recovered from one piece of news when another was flung at me.

As a psychotherapist I have worked with many clients with illnesses, including cancer. I have come to see illness as an invitation to wholeness, in living or in dying. From this perspective, therapy can provide an invaluable opportunity to explore the unfinished business, imbalances in one's life, the unexpressed feelings, and life-style issues that the illness or injury has exposed. Is the person making choices in violation of his or her unique center? What changes does the illness call for?

Every departure from being true to ourselves registers within us; a major departure can lead to illness. The body breaks down to call attention to old destructive patterns and to allow for new patterns to emerge. In this, I believe the therapist can be like a midwife aiding in the birth of new possibilities that will bring the client closer to his or her original center.

A year earlier I had been aware that change was tapping on Dad's door. He had had two crises in a short period—one an altercation at work, the other an automobile accident. After the second, I suggested to Dad that these crises could be signaling the need for change, for creating more balance in his life.

I've learned to appreciate that these signals start out as subtle proddings to pay attention and perhaps change some behavior, but when ignored they will become more dramatic. I urged that he take this into consideration, for if this was true and he ignored the signals, then another even stronger event might force him into change. He listened, but I could tell that he had difficulty even considering any reevaluation of his life. He just wanted things to settle back to normal. I remembered this conversation after I heard the news of his cancer. This was indeed the crisis that would force him to change—in his life or into death.

I was surprised that while one part of me accepted that he was dying, another part seemed unwilling to let him go. A part of me wanted him to fight for his life, so I brought my parents books on different approaches to cancer, hoping that he would explore them until he found one that felt right for him. Perhaps the books would give him his own ideas for and creative approaches to working with the pain and the illness, like those of Norman Cousins. I researched diets that would strengthen his body's immune system, and visualizations and meditations that would be healing physically and spiritually.

But the books lay on the table unread, and I began to realize that my parents did not want my input. They would deal with the illness in their own way. This was ironic to me, because the experience I had gained—through years of meditation, training in death and dying, and working with clients—could have been so much help to my parents in dealing with Dad's pain, illness, and dying. It could have been my gift to them at a time when giving seemed so necessary for all of us. Yet it all seemed in vain. All that experience would now have to help me to accept my own helplessness in the situation and to accept that Dad was going to die in his own way.

The Stages

Whatever initiates us into our grief—the news of a terminal illness, a death, an event years later that triggers a delayed or denied grief—we will pass through several stages on our journey into healing and transformation: shock, descent, and emergence.

Although some move directly into the middle stage, shock is often the first response. Unable to absorb the full impact of the news or death that has just occurred, the mind and body respond with numbness. Life becomes dreamlike and foggy. Edges are blurred and feelings dulled as we are eased into confronting the reality of our loss. For many, shock thus serves a needed role of providing a protective transition into the often overwhelming intensity of the next stage.

As the shock wears off, there seems to be nothing to hold on to as we are swept by a flood of feelings and experiences down into a long, dark passage. Our loss overcomes us, filling us with anguish, longing, relief, anger, depression, numbness, despair, aching, guilt, confusion, and unbearable pain. These feelings often come in waves, arising out of the depths and bowling us over with their intensity; however, there also may be periods of calm, even peace. One never knows what to expect. Conflicting feelings arise simultaneously. In grieving for a parent it is possible to feel both abandoned and released, terrified and exhilarated. Faced with a grief that is not reasonable, rational, consistent, or predictable, the mind struggles for control and understanding, desperately trying to fit the experience into some known mold. It is this sense of being out of control that is so frightening to many in grief.

As we stumble through the darkness, deep within, our grief silently works, breaking down the old structures, churning up unresolved issues, bringing everything into question. Our old visions of the world are shattered, and one by one the old beliefs are challenged: beliefs that our parents are immortal, that they can protect us, that we can always return home. And suddenly our own deaths are one step closer; we are next in line. Life feels fragile and unpredictable. The family is fragmented. The world we had known breaks down.

There is the temptation to put your grief behind you during this long middle phase and return to a normal life, ignoring the forces that seek to break down the world as you had known it. But you will never be the same; you will never be able to return to the life you knew. The death of a parent changes your life unalterably.

You can fight the grief, resisting the feelings, desperately trying to reerect the structures that have tumbled down. But the forces at work here are far greater than willpower. Resisting the inevitable tides of grief is like swimming upstream for days—in spite of your best efforts to make headway, you soon are exhausted and carried downstream.

Many of my clients' current problems can be traced to a grief or loss that was never resolved or healed in the past. Unresolved grief haunts us, silently but insidiously encroaching on our lives years later. I have worked with clients who never grieved over a parent's death as a child—twenty or thirty years later that grief, now disguised, still weighs on them.

When we do not fight the tides of grief but move down into it, the churning, tumultuous forces can go to work, initiating profound changes in our attitudes and perspectives. Finally, after months of disorienting darkness, through an opening in the passage a vast new world glimmers in the sunshine, bidding us to venture forth and explore.

We realize suddenly that we have been transformed in our passage through grief. We are seeing with new eyes, as reflected in a story I often heard at meditation retreats. Achaan Chah, a master of Buddhist meditation living in a forest monastery in Burma, held up a crystal glass, appreciating its exquisite beauty, savoring the colors shimmering in the light. And then he turned to his students and said, "This glass is already broken."

Achaan Chah was able to appreciate fully the beauty of the glass in that moment while simultaneously acknowledging the truth of impermanence.

In grief, we are often faced with lifelong patterns of guarding ourselves from loss, holding back from a full commmitment to life and love because we are afraid of losing what we cherish. Upon the death of a loved one, we often realize that our attempts to protect ourselves have in fact created a deeper pain, that the loss was more excruciating because we held back our love. As we emerge out of our grief into the world again, we are faced with the dilemma of how we can live and love fully while simultaneously embracing the truth of impermanence, of loss. Achaan Chah demonstrated in those few moments with the glass how he had learned to do this.

The tides of grief expose us to the agony of loss and to the inexplicable mystery of death and life. We can gain new respect for the intensity and depth of human emotions, recognizing their power to disrupt our daily lives and routines. In grief, as we confront the pain of holding back from life and from love, we can learn a new appreciation for the fragility of life, the power of love, and the preciousness of each moment. This exposure can deepen us and open us to a life that is bigger, brimming with possibilities on many levels, and fiercely alive.

CHAPTER 4

Creating a Sanctuary

Whether your parent is dying or has died, as you move out of shock and the full impact of your loss begins to hit, you will need to begin implementing strategies for the long middle phase of grief.

Grieving is a complex process, generating many levels of psychic disturbance. Many past societies understood the potential for transformation in a psyche that is shaken up into a chaotic state. They created sacred spaces, sealed off and protected from outside influences, where forces from within the psyche were contained, intensified, and stimulated into activity, ultimately generating healing and transformation.

The Sioux Indian youth went out alone on a vision quest, sitting for days inside a drawn circle, with the commitment that he or she would not step outside until the allotted time had passed. Without the usual outside distractions, the conflicts of the psyche had an opportunity to reveal themselves. Finally, however, the youth might be rewarded with a vision that would become the inspiration for returning to the tribe in a new role, perhaps as a shaman or a healer.

In the ancient art of alchemy, certain elements were combined in a closed vessel and, when activated with heat, supposedly transformed into gold. Psychologist Carl Jung saw this as a fitting image of the process of transformation in the psyche. The contents must be sealed off for a new center to be constellated. Nature has devised her own form of a closed vessel, the egg and the womb, in order to protect the formation of new life in its most vulnerable stages.

Likewise, in many cultures throughout the world ceremonies are enacted within a sacred place that has been delineated. The boundaries keep influences out that might contaminate the ceremony, while containing the forces being activated inside. Although we do not consciously create these boundaries today, there is an implied notion that the circle must not be broken when it is expected that no one will leave the room during an important meeting or leave the table on a special occasion.

In grief there is a tremendous potential of healing and transformation if the powerful forces that are already activated are contained and protected from outside influences. To serve this purpose you can create a sanctuary, a safe place where you can go each day to honor and experience your grief.

In your sanctuary, you have the opportunity to work with the intense forces and emotions that have been aroused in grief. You may want to explore and express these feelings and thoughts, whether in tears, reflection, or writing. You may use the time to resolve unfinished business with your parent, healing the old wounds, accessing the love, and preparing to say goodbye. You may need to use this time to work on the issues that surface with your other parent or your siblings. There are many new perspectives to integrate and questions to ask. The sanctuary becomes a nurturing womb where you are cradled in your suffering while new life is germinated.

The first step is to find and establish a sanctuary; whether it is in your home or in nature, it must be a quiet place where you will not be interrupted. You may want to set up an altar where you can place pictures of your parent, special objects, candles, or flowers. What you choose may change over time. I originally placed on the shelf over my bed a picture of my father next to a small statue of St. Francis and a lucky coin my father had treasured. Over time I added some special rocks and a small redwood cone, as my connection to the earth grew stronger.

After you have prepared your sanctuary, set aside a period of time each day to be there. Most of my clients have settled upon an effective rhythm of an hour a day, although in practice this often ranges from half an hour to an hour each day. This is a special time, devoted to your grief. It is important that you not be interrupted or pulled away. Put on the answering machine or take the phone off the hook; put a note on the door. Protected from outside disturbances, you are now ready to open to the experience of your grief.

I have emphasized to my clients the importance of finding a rhythm of entering into the grief totally for a block of time each day and then letting it go, moving back into the stream of life. This is hard to do but well worth the effort. It has not worked well for my clients to immerse themselves in grief for hours and hours a day—the experience becomes overwhelming. Nor has it worked to proceed with one's daily activities without setting aside times to experience and honor the grief. Then one goes through the day in a dazed state, weighed down by a grief that is always in the background, unable to heal and unable to give attention to the activity at hand. The grief responds well to short, focused periods of full attention.

At first you may dread the time alone, for this is often a frightening experience during grief. The death of a parent does make us feel excruciatingly alone in the world. Perhaps we hoped that someone—our parents, a lover, our child—would save us from confronting this reality, but with the death of a parent we are jolted awake. We realize, "I've come into this world alone and I will die alone. I'm all that I've got." We may desperately attempt to avoid this painful new awareness.

Many turn to friends during grief so as not to feel so terrifyingly alone. This brings a desperation to the encounters that fosters rejection and clinging. The effort to escape one's aloneness in grief can backfire into major crises.

On the other hand, if even for small periods you can open to the experience of the aloneness, entering into its very heart, you will find in the dark space of that inexhaustible void a way back to a source of life from within. It is at this source that you come upon the resources to move through the passage of grief and ultimately to transform the experience into a healing.

Then you will be ready for taking the step toward new life and love. In a rhythm of contact and withdrawal that even your cells participate in, the turning inward naturally prepares you to turn outward again. Clark Moustakas wrote in *Loneliness and Love* that "in the lonely hours the return to one's self brings with it a readiness to return to others" (p. 56).

If you feel trepidation about being alone with your grief, begin your sanctuary time with only ten or fifteen minutes. As you feel more comfortable, realizing the healing potential, you can gradually extend the time.

As you sit in your chosen place, take some time just to be with yourself, doing nothing. Sit quietly, breathing in silence. There is more to doing nothing than meets the eye, as I have learned from years of meditation. When you allow yourself to do nothing, new connections can take place; the pieces of your life have the opportunity to settle and integrate. Each experience and reaction does not need to be analyzed and understood; a deeper layer of integration occurs without effort if you can open up to the space for it to happen.

Tune in to and acknowledge what you are feeling. Embrace whatever is happening in the moment, without judgment. If feelings surface, let them flow; give yourself full permission to cry or express your anger if you want to. If you feel numb, bring your full awareness to that experience, without judging it. While at first you may think that nothing is going on inside, you'll notice that numbness brings its own set of experiences and sensations.

Give yourself the permission to be however you are in this moment. This is the gift of love to yourself. In grief you need your love, your tenderness, your protection—indeed, as Stephen Levine emphasized in his retreats, much of our grieving arises from the realization of how little room there is for ourselves in our own hearts.

Like many of my clients, you may initially feel some resistance to creating a sanctuary for yourself. It is difficult with all the stresses and demands of daily life to set that time aside. However, this is a critical step. Start with ten minutes if you need to, and build from there as you experience the benefits for yourself. You will be amazed, as many clients have been, at the dramatic and subtle shifts that begin to take place.

Throughout the following chapters, we will turn to other possibilities to explore during the sanctuary time that can foster a deepening and bring healing and integration to the experience of grief.

CHAPTER 5

The Dream that Broke the Impasse

As the outer channels for finding some solution to the crisis of my father's illness were blocked, I turned within. I made a commitment to meditate daily. I hoped that this time spent in meditation would facilitate a healing so that I could move through this crisis with an open heart, accepting and loving my father as he was. Although I did not define it as such then, I was creating a sanctuary, a protected space in which to explore my grief.

For years, meditation had carried me through many crises, as I sat in silence watching the flow of my breath, the thoughts and sensations arising and passing away moment to moment. The clarity and spaciousness of mind that I experienced enabled me to enter daily activities with awareness and to face challenges with a larger perspective.

But this time, the meditations felt consistently arid. My mind could concentrate but my heart felt closed. I began to panic. How was I going to make it through this crisis if all the old resources didn't work? Edward Whitmont wrote in *The Symbolic Quest* that the process of becoming whole often begins with confronting an insoluble problem, one that seems to have no way out. When the old means of finding solutions fail, "sooner or later dreams or fantasies will appear which not only show but initiate possibilities of development" that might not otherwise occur to us (p. 308). At that time I was too caught up in my panic to be comforted by this perspective; however, images that began to guide me in new directions appeared in my dreams.

Since childhood I have had enormous respect for the power
of dreams. I started my first dream journal in fifth grade. In
rereading these journals I have seen how my dreams are a guiding
and healing force in my life, nudging me to confront unresolved
issues, calling attention to aspects of my personality that I would
otherwise ignore, inspiring me to realize my potential.

In the midst of my confusion, I had a vivid dream from which
I awakened in an uneasy and deeply disturbed state.

> I am in a pool listening to a group reciting a play
> when the water starts to drain out. I climb out and
> join the monks as they begin to chant and walk in
> meditation. In an adjoining room, I can see what looks
> like a dead man reciting the Buddhist precepts; as I
> watch him, he seems to harden into a statue with only
> the lips moving.
> A blind woman walks in with a seeing eye dog,
> her powerful presence immediately drawing my
> attention. A free spirit, she visits the monastery at her
> own discretion, the monks receiving her as one of their
> community but expecting from her none of the
> traditional roles.
> Sitting down before the head monk, she engages
> him in an animated dialogue in a foreign language.
> Drawn to their conversation even though I cannot
> understand it, I move closer and sit on the floor before
> them. The woman suddenly turns and focuses all her
> intensity on me. She looks deeply into my eyes and
> says, "You are very nervous." I feel unnerved but very
> drawn to her.

Still feeling the powerful impact of these images, I was struck
by the deadness portrayed in the monastery. The water draining out of the pool and the dead man's mechanical recitations
seemed to hint that the psyche was withdrawing its energy from
this area. Perhaps the form of the Buddhist meditation I had
practiced for eleven years was not going to be my primary support through my father's illness. The thought frightened me,
since it confirmed the unsettling sense I had already had that the

old resources were not going to help me through this crisis. Where else could I turn?

Then my attention was drawn to the image of the woman in the dream. She brought new life to the scene, exuding a freedom and a power that was intriguing to me. And she seemed to see with an inner vision right into me, cutting through my masks and fears. She saw me just as I was and was not afraid to confront me with that truth.

This woman began to appear in many of my subsequent dreams. Her appearance became a turning point; she guided me into new resources and new worlds. Though she looked different each time, she always projected the same powerful presence. In one dream I had to go through a series of tests, one of which was to climb a very tall ladder that had slippery rungs. So as not to panic, I had to pay close attention to grabbing hold of each rung. The woman followed close behind me, reassuring me and giving me support as I made the difficult transition to the platform.

In another dream the same woman encouraged me to work with her on a project she had undertaken, a project that she vaguely referred to as having to do with death and spirit. In another she appeared as a nun throwing little crystal stones over my hands, watching carefully for my reaction as though this were some sort of test. In yet another I sat in front of her as I had done in the monastery dream, and she proceeded to encourage me to practice sending energy to her. I was shocked at the power coming through my hands as I leaned toward her. In still another dream she took a group of us through a series of tests and taught us different skills. In one of these tests she threw us so forcefully into a pool that we were propelled to the bottom and had to swim to the surface.

In all these visions and dreams, I was clearly aware that this woman was a powerful guide, drawing me toward an entirely new level of awareness. Though I did not yet always grasp the point of her tests or the lessons she was intending me to learn, I was convinced that she was there to help and I made the decision to trust and honor her.

CHAPTER 6

The Power of Dreams to Heal

Grief gives you a precious opportunity to work with the guidance and gifts from the deep strata of the psyche, the unconscious. As grief draws you down into the dark recesses of the underworld, it brings you into closer contact with the unconscious than you ordinarily have. Vivid dreams may occur that stun you with their power. These dreams can be an invaluable source of guidance and healing at this chaotic time when the ego is floundering.

As a parent is dying, dreams can help one navigate through the inevitable crises and difficulties, as well as prepare for the death itself. After a parent has died, there can be a comforting sense of continuity in dreaming about the parent while one is struggling to accept the loss. Throughout grief, dreams can help to make conscious whatever is being repressed or minimized, thus providing reliable feedback on how effectively one is grieving.

Dreaming is a universal experience; we all dream, even though we may not remember what we dream. I have heard many clients protest that they don't dream; these same clients come into my office weeks later with dreams scribbled in notebooks or on backs of envelopes.

It is worth the effort to attempt to remember and record dreams. Their healing power is so great that a discarded dream is like gold cast away. Dreams confront us with the truth about ourselves, a truth emerging from the deep layers of our psyche.

The wise words of the historian Mircea Eliade in his book

Shamanism depict the power of dreams: "It is in dreams that the pure sacred life is entered and direct relations with the gods, spirits and ancestral souls are re-established" (p. 103). In most cultures throughout history, dreams have been respected and looked to for guidance and inspiration. In the shamanic traditions the shaman often received his or her calling through a dream and looked to dreams for information regarding healing and cosmology. Dreams are scattered throughout the Bible, many playing pivotal roles in major decisions and events. In ancient Greece, healing was very much connected with dreams; at the temple of Asklepius at Epidauros the gods visited the supplicants in their dreams while they slept. In the modern Western world the respect for dreams dwindled, until it was revived in the work of Sigmund Freud and Carl Jung.

Carl Jung spoke of the unconscious as that subterranean area of a person's psyche that is a storehouse of memories. The personal unconscious contains all the fears, experiences, and fantasies that a person may not wish to face because they are incompatible with self-concepts or are contrary to societal mores. The collective unconscious is thought to be the common substratum of all individuals, containing the collected knowledge of humankind. Dreams are the link with this storehouse. Speaking through the language of imagery, they remind us of what we are rejecting and what we need to accept in order to become whole. They can also put us in touch with ancient wisdom.

Some people say they don't have dreams. It is likely rather that the dreams never quite reach the threshold of consciousness. In order to remember dreams one has to establish a relationship with the unconscious by being willing to listen to the feedback and wisdom inherent in each dream. It is also important to record dreams as soon as possible after awakening. The very act of recording acknowledges the dream.

However, even once the dream has been retrieved, there is the danger that the conscious mind will subject the dream to such analysis and judgment that the spirit of the dream will be lost. That spirit needs to be respected by allowing the dream and its images to work on us, to gently move us in ways often incomprehensible to the rational mind. Whether the dream is understood or not, it still influences the dreamer.

Gradually the images may begin to shed light on different aspects of one's life. The unconscious speaks to us through the language of imagery. We bring to each image a wealth of associations that may illuminate what the unconscious is communicating. In addition, an image may need to be explored against the backdrop of mythological and archetypal associations. For example, in dreaming about a snake, you may have personal associations and feelings about a snake that you bring to the image— perhaps fear or revulsion, or perhaps memories of playing with snakes as a young child. It may also be helpful to be aware that in mythology the snake is a symbol of healing and transformation.

The first step in dreamwork is to remember dreams. You may want to say to your unconscious before going to sleep, "I am open to whatever my unconscious wants to communicate through my dreams. I would like to have a dream tonight that I will remember." If you are struggling with a particular problem, you can ask for a dream that gives you insights into that problem. Some have found it helpful to go through a process before falling asleep of imagining falling asleep, dreaming a dream, awakening, and writing it all down.

Keep a pen and paper by your bed and immediately upon awakening write down whatever fragment of the dream you remember. It is similar to pulling a fish out of the water: if you catch just the tail, often it is possible to pull the rest of the fish along with it. Many of my clients have hesitated to write down a fragment, deeming it unworthy. That fragment can stimulate the memory of the rest of the dream; even if it doesn't, that fragment alone can often yield rich insights when explored.

I value and actively use the feedback and guidance of the unconscious through dreams in my therapy practice. The first dream a new client brings me is often a clue to the direction of the work we will explore together. Subsequent dreams give us feedback as to whether we are on track and whether certain areas are in the process of healing or are still needing more work.

For example, one of my clients shared a dream of a pool full of fish in her first session. The water was draining out and the fish were in danger of losing their lives. As we explored the images, she expressed concern that the water was flowing away; she sensed that this referred to what was happening to her own life force. Indeed, she was struggling with an undiagnosed illness. In the dream, as in her life, a crisis was at hand, threatening her vitality.

As she discussed her associations with the fish, memories began to surface of her strict religious upbringing, an experience that had traumatized her. As a result, for years she had not known where to turn to meet her spiritual needs, needs that now she could not ignore. The dream brought home to her that this was not only a physical crisis but a spiritual one as well.

In response to this powerful dream, our subsequent sessions focused on ways she could explore the spiritual dimensions of her life while healing the wounds of the past. Only a few weeks later a dream confirmed our direction. In this dream she was swimming with dolphins in the ocean, and it was a joyful and liberating experience. She had reconnected with the water of life, her spiritual base.

Grief churns up the deepest layers of the psyche, bringing to the surface the unresolved issues that silently sabotage our lives. Our dreams inform us of the presence of these issues and offer guidance on how to heal. When these dreams are ignored, they can repeat themselves or appear in more dramatic forms, perhaps developing into nightmares. When one awakens from a nightmare in a sweat, terrified, it is more difficult to put the dream out of one's consciousness.

Many of my clients have experienced disturbing dreams and nightmares in the months following the death of a parent. One client, Celia, had nightmares of a man breaking into her house for months after her father's death. She would awaken feeling frightened and apprehensive that a stranger was indeed in her house.

In our sessions we explored different approaches to this dream, but it persisted in its same form. It has been my experience that the unconscious responds readily to any work on a dream, providing feedback through subsequent dreams. If the dreams change, there may be new material emerging. If they do not, the unconscious seems to be saying, "Stay with this a while longer. There is something here that needs more attention and awareness."

Weeks later Celia was growing so frustrated with this nightmare that she expressed a willingness to confront the man in her dreams. Before this she had not been willing even to consider this. In our session, I asked her to close her eyes and imagine herself back in the environment of the dream. I continued to question her (What are you seeing? What are you doing? What are you wearing? What does the room look like? How are you feeling? What do you hear? What is the temperature of the room?) until she felt that she was fully present in the dream, experiencing it with all her senses in her imagination. Then I suggested that she return to the point at which she would usually awaken, when the man was entering her bedroom. She allowed him to approach.

For a brief moment she was able to set aside her assumption that he was going to hurt her; she asked him what he wanted. He softened, the threatening quality to his demeanor vanishing, and said, "I've just wanted to talk with you. For months I've wanted to talk with you, but you have ignored me." And they began to talk, their conversation revealing many new insights into her relationship to this inner male presence. He then asked for a commitment that over the next few weeks she would spend time each day visiting with him in her imagination.

She proceeded to do this, talking with him daily before she went to sleep. These talks inspired her to question and evaluate her attitudes and behavior in relationships and brought to light many unresolved issues with her father and with her former husband. The nightmares ceased.

Celia's father's death had activated deep psychic material that had been conditioning her relationships with men. The dreams demanded her attention and then, when she was willing to listen, provided guidance for healing.

This common dream theme of a man or woman breaking into a house has also sometimes activated memories of sexual abuse. One woman dreamed of her father climbing through the window of her bedroom, and upon awakening vividly remembered childhood incidents in which her father crept into her bedroom at night and fondled her.

Dreams can also initiate a new awareness of the dysfunctional patterns within the family, many of which come to light with a new, often disturbing clarity after a parent's death. For example, after attending his mother's funeral service, a client had a series of dreams in which his mother was extremely drunk, dreams that broke through his denial of her alcoholism.

On the other hand, dreams can provide comfort and can generate feelings of deep peace during the troubled times before and after a parent's death. One woman joined one of my groups to grieve her father's death. She also wanted to prepare for the death of her mother who had cancer. Having lost one parent, she felt very anxious and fearful about losing the other. After one of our meetings, she had a dream in which her mother told her: "It is my time. I'm ready to go. I want to be with my husband." The profound peace and acceptance with which she awakened stayed with her through the days leading to her mother's death—two weeks later.

Another client felt troubled by many questions after her father's death: What is death? What has happened to my father? Although she had been very close to her father, she did not experience any contact with him after he died, not even in her dreams. This disturbed her and made her question whether consciousness really does continue after death, as she had read in many books. Then months later she had a dream in which her father had been taken away to prison. She set out to find him and, after a long search, reached a driveway that led to the prison. However, to her amazement, the driveway led to a pristine wooded area on a gently sloping hill. She thought to herself, "How could such a beautiful place be a prison?"

As she surveyed the woods, she knew intuitively that the prisoners were kept inside the trees. One imposing tree towered over her. Filled with a sense of love for this tree, she felt impelled to embrace its trunk and then to climb it. As she settled on the upper limbs, she was surrounded by sweet spring air, an expanse of brilliant blue sky and, off in the distance, the ocean sparkling in the sunlight. In that place she felt complete; she felt that everything that had troubled her was resolved, even the need to find her father. She felt comforted by the realization that her father—in death—and she—in life—could experience that peace that goes beyond all understanding.

During your sanctuary time you may want to write down the dreams from the previous night in a journal. I record brief notes on a scratch pad by my bed upon awakening from a dream and then record the dream more fully in my journal later in the day. Just writing the dream down often stimulates insights.

When writing the dream in your journal, write it in the present tense, as though it were happening now. This keeps the dream alive and enables you to go back into it. When you have recorded the dream, give it a name based on some major aspect of the dream. These names provide easy access to dreams written in your journal, a few words triggering the memory of the entire dream. These are some of the names I have given my dreams: The Sunfish, The Ruby, Ann's Birthday, Walk with Stephen, New House, Lightning, Hidden Spring.

Then sit with the dream, letting it work on you. Be willing to let the images come alive, without interpreting them. Then you can explore the relation this dream has to your present situation, the conflicts and unresolved situations in the dream, the resolutions presented in the dream, the new choices that the dream may inspire.

There is no one meaning to the dream, since the dream works at many levels at once. James Hillman, author of boldly innovative books on dreams, wrote in *The Dream and the Underworld,* "If we think back on any dream that has been important to us, as time passes and the more we reflect on it, the more we discover in it. . . . This unending, embracing depth is one way dreams show their love" (p. 200).

CHAPTER 7

Keeping a Journal

A journal becomes an invaluable resource during grief, not only to record dreams but also to explore the many faces of grief. You may want to keep a daily record of all that you are experiencing; as the jumbled thoughts and feelings come to the surface, they can be written down in a stream of consciousness without editing. There is often a sense of relief in doing this, as though a burden had been lifted. In grief there are so many conflicting and overwhelming feelings and experiences that to set them down on paper is very cleansing and comforting. Reflecting on what you have just written may reveal a new order beginning to take form in the chaos.

Keeping a journal is not only valuable at the time you are writing it; it also gives you the opportunity to reread your experiences at a later time when you have more time to integrate them. Your memory alone may not be reliable, since it has a tendency to revise and edit in situations of overwhelming intensity. You may be certain you will never forget some events and feelings, only to find that the journal is the only resource for remembering them.

Many find it healing to reread their journals on the anniversary of a parent's death; with each passing year the events around the death are seen through new eyes. Some return to their journal to explore and heal a particularly painful aspect of their parent's illness or death.

The following journal exercise can be very illuminating and healing in grief. Parts of it were inspired by the material in Ira Progoff's book, *At a Journal Workshop*.

Before you begin to write, close your eyes and sit in silence, becoming aware of the steady rhythm of your breathing, breathing in and breathing out. With each breath move your attention deeper within, embracing more and more of your inner experience. Feel the movement of feelings and thoughts within you. Let go of whatever was happening last week or yesterday; move past any concepts you have held of grief, and open to the present moment. Then record whatever you are experiencing and observing, without editing.

As the days pass, you will notice how grief is a constantly changing prism, with thoughts and feelings creating new patterns of light and dark. Once you can let go of your previous ideas and concepts and are willing to explore and investigate, you will discover that each moment is subtly different than the last.

Now close your eyes and bring your attention to this time of your life, your passage through grief. Feel the movement of that grief from its first stirrings to the present moment. How did it begin? How did it unfold? The grief has carried you through many phases, crises, events, and inner experiences. Record whatever you observe.

Then turn your attention within again, and explore the qualities of your grief at this time. What color is it? What shape? What temperature is it? What consistency? What weight? How does it feel? Open your eyes and write about what you have experienced.

CHAPTER 8

Gleams of Another World

I began to explore letting go of the familiar forms of meditation I had practiced for many years, simply opening myself to whatever might emerge as I sat quietly. One day, as soon as I closed my eyes, a flood of rich, clear images was waiting. Throughout my years of Buddhist practice I had been taught not to pursue imagery in my meditations; I had allowed my imaginal world free reign only in dreams and in active imagination work in therapy. So this was a new experience for me.

> *That afternoon I see in my mind's eye glistening dolphins weaving golden threads as they delicately carry them in their mouths. These threads encircle the earth in a protective web of gold. I can see holes in this web; the dolphins are diving in and out of the ocean, reweaving these areas as on a giant loom.*

I was stunned at the power and clarity of these images. I felt that I had moved into another world. I was so intrigued that the very next day I sat again and closed my eyes, allowing myself to open to imagery just as I had done on the first day.

> *Immediately I see mountain ranges all around me, high, steep, bare mountains. Before me is a steep cliff with a ladder hewn in the rock. I climb it to a cave entrance hidden partway up the rock face.*
> *As I enter the cave, an old man, dressed in a simple white loincloth, greets me. He seems to be expecting me*

*and mysteriously informs me that I am being prepared, as
though this information should provide some comfort.
Without saying another word, he leads me to a low
doorway to the right that opens into a smaller cave.*

*I sense this is an inner sanctuary. The walls are stone
and the space is sparsely furnished with a rustic wood
table and bench. On the floor a bulging red blanket stirs,
and a woman emerges from her womblike shelter. Her
power is so intense that I have difficulty focusing my eyes.*

*My heart sees what my eyes cannot, and I know this is
the woman of my recent dreams. I kneel at her feet,
cherishing these moments with her. I tell her how I have
been struggling with my parents' approach to my father's
illness and ask her help.*

*Without saying a word, she places Dad in a chair in
the middle of a red circle drawn on the floor, touching
him with a feather that sends bolts of lightning through
his body. She focuses on a spot in the middle of his body.
Then, with light, swift strokes, she brushes him off. Red
erupts through the floor and through Dad's body.*

*A rain of silvery light falls over us. The woman turns
to me. "The Creator embraces all things without
judgment. Your parents are meeting this crisis in their own
way." She moves closer, whispering softly, "My child, you
are being prepared. You have to burn now."*

When I opened my eyes, I felt renewed, inspired, and awed.
The images had tumbled forth as though they had been simply
waiting for the door to open. I knew in my heart that I had
touched upon a wellspring of vital power and healing that invited
me to visit again.

The next day, upon closing my eyes I found myself climbing
the ladder up the steep stone face.

*I enter the cave. To my disappointment there is no one
there. I look around. The cave is illuminated by the light
of many candles on a stone altar to my left. Before me an
old trunk rests against the stone wall. To my right there is
a faded wall hanging. Next to it is the doorway to the
smaller cave. I crouch down as I pass through.*

*The woman emerges from under her red blanket and
we greet one another warmly. Deep lines encircle her dark
eyes. Her strong, wrinkled hands clasp mine as she peers
searchingly into the hidden chambers of my psyche. Then
she speaks: "You can call me Belatha." Mesmerized by
her, I falter as I attempt to respond.*

*She places her right hand in my palm, gesturing for me
to look into the large, green emerald of her ring. I fall into
green waves, swirling into green.*

*Suddenly I am standing on a ledge in an unfamiliar
landscape studded with rocks and scrubby vegetation. I
jump off the ledge and begin climbing along the rocks.*

*Sensing a presence nearby, I look up and see
crouching above me a large yellow-striped tiger pinning
me with its gold eyes. Telepathically he tells me that I
need to learn courage from him. I feel his strength
flooding my cells, cells rearranging to become tiger. I
watch and wait in stillness, my great striped paws
stretched in relaxed anticipation on the hot rock.*

*Then I am back in the cave with Belatha. I ask about
my father. Instantly I can feel my cells rearranging into
new patterns, my body shifting, bending over, in response
to the grabbing pain I feel in my neck. I have become Dad
as I look down in a whirlpool; I feel dark and depressed. I
call for help from my guide. Immediately a rain of energy
falls over me, my body jolting in response. My neck jerks
violently, and then my chest and abdomen. Then I am
floating in a luminous space of peace and stillness. Am I
dying?*

My eyes opened to the threads of the familiar rust-colored
carpet. My body ached, my clothes were soaked with sweat. I lay
on my side in a heap, quite a distance from the pillow I had been
sitting on at the beginning of my meditation.

As I reflected on the images I had just experienced, I was
struck again with their extreme clarity. I had the disturbing
thought that I had entered another world. This world seemed to
have its own geography, its own inhabitants. I had the sense that
I could return to that cave again. The experience of that world
felt very natural when I was in it; it was only when I came back to

my everyday reality that I felt confused and disoriented. Now I was motivated by the strong sense that the experience of this other world could help me in the crisis with my father.

As I lay on the carpet, I remembered reading about a workshop on the shamanic journey given by American anthropologist and shaman Michael Harner, author of *The Way of the Shaman*. Perhaps this workshop could give me the tools and support to continue my exploration of this new world.

I signed up that day and a week later was sitting in a circle of fifty people at Esalen Institute, listening intently to a talk by Michael Harner, his stories punctuated by his hearty laughter. Michael started out by emphasizing to his audience that shamanism is not reserved for the elite; he would be teaching a method over the weekend that would enable each person to gain first-hand knowledge and experience of shamanism.

He then defined a shaman as a person who has the ability to contact an ordinarily hidden reality while in an altered state of consciousness. Michael stressed over and over that this reality, which he calls "nonordinary reality," is not to be confused with the one we experience in ordinary consciousness. They coexist, neither negating the other, each real in its own way. He shared how his explorations into nonordinary reality had enriched his life; the magic, mystery, and limitless possibilities he experienced there were an ongoing source of wisdom, awe, and excitement. He could never again feel trapped in a narrow, limited existence.

As he spoke, I reflected on the places I had visited and the guides I had met in my recent excursions into this other reality. This was just the beginning of my exploration; already I had learned so much, been profoundly moved by the love of animals and guides, and accessed resources for healing. I felt empowered at a time of great helplessness in the circumstances of my life. So many new perspectives were opening up within at a time when outer options seemed so limited.

Michael then proceeded to teach a simple method for journeying into this nonordinary reality, a method used successfully by shamans for thousands of years. The very structure of the journey provides a clear distinction between the worlds, a defin-

ite passage from one to the other so that there is no danger of
mixing or confusing the two worlds. Aided by the steady beat of
the drum or by the use of psychedelic drugs, the shaman, sitting
or lying in darkness with eyes closed, leaves the known world
through a hole and travels down a tunnel that opens onto a new
and yet ancient universe. He or she explores that world, mapping
it so that certain places can be found again on other journeys.

After Michael had guided us down the tunnel a few times, he
set us the task of finding a guardian who could protect and guide
us on our journey. This usually takes the form of an animal,
known as a *power animal*. Thus the shaman reestablishes in this
inner world a bond and communication that existed in primi-
tive cultures. This animal is a source of great power. In fact, it
is a widespread belief in shamanic societies that if a power animal leaves a person, he or she will certainly become ill and
perhaps die.

As he discussed power animals, and the probability that
many of us had already had contact with them through significant dreams or encounters, I thought of the tiger that I had met
recently. Then I remembered with a start the feeling of recognition upon meeting him. He had come to me in two powerful dreams seven years apart, as though he had been trying to
contact me.

Ten years before I had had a dream in which I was sleeping
on a platform in a field. In the middle of the night I was awakened
by the feeling of a nearby presence. Two sets of glowing, yellow
eyes were watching me in the darkness. As I looked closer I saw
two tigers, and yet I felt no fear.

In the second dream, seven years later, a tiger leaped out of
the night, threatening to kill my cat. I moved quickly to protect
the cat, provoking the tiger to come after me instead. This led to a
direct encounter in which I asserted my power and warned it not
to threaten me. As the dream ended, I was holding the tiger's
attention with my eyes, wondering what to do next.

I was shaken when I met my second power animal, the wolf,
because as a child, I had had repeated experiences of imagining
wolves under my bed. I couldn't call out or move for fear of their

attacking me. I would lie in bed for hours, sweating and trembling with fear.

In my late twenties, these wolves appeared in a very different manner in a dream: I was in a meadow, sitting on a platform in a rustic wooden chair that seemed to be a throne. I was surrounded by adoring wolves with whom I was communicating telepathically and for whom I felt great love.

Another contact was made in a workshop in response to an exercise in which we were to reenter a childhood dream. In my imagination I began to experience the sense of danger as I lay on the bed, feeling very small and helpless as I sensed the presence of wolves under my bed. Suddenly a wolf appeared from under the bed and rested its head tenderly on the blanket, saying, "I am your ally. I'm here to protect you." I stroked its great, soft head very gently and lovingly as tears flooded down my cheeks. I knew then that I had always been protected.

Then, sketching out for us the three worlds (Upper, Middle, and Lower) that we could expect to find in nonordinary reality, and providing us with a few basic guidelines, Michael encouraged us to use the journeys to make our own discoveries. His final advice was that we enter these other worlds with a purpose and bring back the power and knowledge attained to help and serve others.

That workshop, along with my own reading of material related to shamanism and imaginal psychology, gave me a framework within which to explore the world I had stumbled into during those first few experiences. In my mind's eye, I began leaving my everyday consciousness from a pool along the river at Esalen, following the tunnel and exploring the world that opened out for the duration of the drumming. Then I hurried back up the tunnel and splashed out of the pool. I met one of my teachers deep in the Lower World.

> *The tiger leads me through darkness down to an underground forest. Hidden in the gnarled roots of a gigantic tree is a small opening with a rustic sign carved over it in a strange lettering. As the tiger looks confidently*

toward this, I step over the earthen threshold, wondering what I will find.

A tall man is waiting as though he expected me, his weathered hands extended in welcome. White hair cascades over his shoulders like turbulent rapids, and yet his skin is as smooth and clear as a child's, his body strong and straight as an athlete's. He is imposing in stature, yet he emanates gentleness and inspires trust.

I move forward to take his hands, filled instantly with love for this stranger. I feel in some unexplainable way that I know him already, that this is a reunion rather than a first meeting.

In a low, resonant voice, he introduces himself as Xan and acknowledges how difficult this crisis is for me. He emphasizes how much loss and how many disappointments I will experience as I learn to let the Spirit live through me. Placing his hands softly on my head, he begins pouring energy into me, my body shaking with tremors as it tries to adjust to the power surging through it.

Opening my eyes after this journey, I was stunned. Xan had been so real to me. I had seen him so clearly, touched him, felt the power of the energy in his hands. As I lay on the floor, workshop participants stirring around me, my body was still humming with that energy. My heart was pounding hard against the walls of my chest, with excitement and love. This love I felt for Xan was overwhelming and yet comforting.

In all these journeys, I had the sense that while my experiences were taking place in an imaginal world, the lessons I was being offered there could be carried back to my everyday world. I did not yet know how these lessons were going to apply to my daily challenges, but I knew that the time had come when I needed the support, love, and knowledge of the guides I had met in this place.

CHAPTER 9

Awakening the Inner Senses

My own shamanic journeys taught me that without a shadow of a doubt there is within each of us an invisible world of infinite possibilities that coexists with the outer, physical world. We perceive this hidden reality through a kind of sixth sense, the imagination. Shamanic traditions have explored this reality for thousands of years. Unfortunately, imagination has been denigrated and belittled in the West; we tend to distrust it, as evidenced by the commonly used expression, "That's just your imagination." As a result, we have lost the ability to access this invisible world.

However, the visionaries of our culture have persisted in their attempts to restore imagination to its rightful place in the human psyche and as a bridge between the worlds. Carl Jung described imagination as the "mother of all possibilities" and used it extensively in his work as a link between the inner and outer worlds. Jungian analyst and author June Singer emphasized in an article in *Gnosis* magazine that we can use imagination to see through the visible world into one that is mysterious and invisible. "It requires a different kind of perception to see into that world, because it contains the mystery of how life was before we had any memory of it. . . . It's maybe the world of the unconscious but it's more than that because it's not only psychological but very real" (pp. 20–21).

James Hillman bases his approach to psychology on the reality of the imagination, writing in *Re-Visioning Psychology:*

"To live psychologically is to imagine things . . . our existence is imagination" (p. 23). In the field of medicine, Jeanne Achterberg, author of *Imagery in Healing: Shamanism and Modern Medicine,* explores the roots of healing with the imagination in shamanism and proposes its effective use in modern medicine. "Healing with the gifts of the imagination, long the province of the shaman, has taken an extraordinary new direction. No longer are these talents considered the exclusive territory of a privileged few; now they are accessible to all" (p. 111).

Psychologist Kenneth Ring, author of *Heading Toward Omega,* sees this use of imagination as the next evolutionary step for humankind. He shared these words at a conference I attended in San Francisco: "What we are witnessing is the beginning stages of the shamanizing of humanity, and thereby of humanity finding its way back to its true home in the realm of the imagination where we will live in mythic time and no longer just in historical time. In other words, in this period of apparently accelerating evolutionary pressure, it is the case that these two worlds may be drawing closer to one another so that, like the traditional shaman, we too will find it easy to cross the bridge between the worlds and live comfortably in both of them." We too can learn to bridge these worlds and gain access to the resources, healing, and guidance we need during the critical time of grief. There is so little preparation and support in our culture for grieving, yet within us are resources beyond our wildest imagination.

In preparing to explore this hidden reality, it is essential to learn to trust and use the imagination. The following series of exercises was designed for this purpose. While the first exercise activates the inner faculties of perception and awakens the inner senses, subsequent exercises focus on inspiring and stimulating the flow of imagination without the interference of judgment. Finally, you will learn the basic steps of entering and leaving another reality.

The following exercise is intended to guide you in awakening your inner senses so that you can experience the inner world in all its wonder and richness. Most of us have lost the full use of our senses in ordinary reality—we don't experience things fully. Our senses have been dulled. In awakening the inner senses, you will probably discover that your outer senses become more activated as well.

Close your eyes and imagine yourself standing in a rose garden. All around you are roses of every conceivable color, in all stages of blooming. This is a rich feast for the eyes. As you are enjoying the delights of this garden, the sound of birds singing fills your ears. Listen; let your ears awaken to the subtle sounds all around you—perhaps the breeze rustling the leaves or the sound of an animal nearby.

Now choose one bush that draws your attention. Walk toward it. Examine it closely—notice the patterns of the leaves, the colors and shapes of the roses, the structure of the bush itself, the texture of the soil from which it grows.

Now lean forward to smell one of the roses, the sweet perfume filling your nostrils. Savor this smell. Reach out toward one of the roses, touching it very gently, feeling the soft petals. Close your eyes and concentrate on this sense of touch. Let your fingertips revel in the sensations of touching and stroking the rose. Open your eyes again and drink in with your eyes the beauty of that rose.

Watch that rose as its petals begin to unfold, turning back to reveal another layer of petals within. Layer by layer the rose is blooming to reveal its center. And at its very center something begins to take form. Watch it emerge, without interfering. You may not understand what it means; just let it be as it is.

Another important step in preparing to enter the imaginal world is to stimulate and inspire the flow of imagination, learning to let it unfold by itself without judgment or criticism. Writing one's own fairy tale is a powerful exercise that works with this. As I have discussed previously, imagination is the medium through which we perceive an ordinarily hidden reality. However, due to our conditioning, many of us are skeptical of and resistant to working with imagination. I have watched the look of panic or dismay cross the faces of many of my clients when I have suggested that they write or tell me a fairy tale. "I couldn't do that!" Most of the clients doubt their ability to access their imagination but are shocked by the power that emerges from their stories.

I was introduced to this exercise years ago in a workshop with the Jungian analyst Alice Howell. I have used variations ever since with staggering success.

In preparation for your fairy tale you will want to create five piles of words on index cards or small pieces of paper. One pile will have magical objects: sword, crown, seed, egg, cross, chalice, drum, arrow, star, ring, stone, rose, pearl, key, talisman. Add whatever other objects come to mind. The next pile will be places, such as village, tunnel, valley, forest, cave, desert, garden, meadow, church, mountain, sea, bazaar. Then create a pile of animals, such as dolphin, cat, dog, turtle, owl, sparrow, raven, fox, pig, crocodile, snake, eagle, fish, horse, lion, tiger, bear, whale. Then people, such as grandfather, grandmother, father, mother, girl, boy, child, queen, king, prince, princess, old woman, priest, priestess, old man, maiden. Then magical people and creatures, such as gnome, dragon, soothsayer, fairy, goblin, monster, troll, giant, dwarf, mermaid, monster, angel, witch, wizard, unicorn, sorceress. Add your own ideas to each category.

With the piles face down, select one card from each. The five words that you then hold in your hand are the words that you will weave into your fairy tale. You will want to start with the magical invocation "Once upon a time . . ."

The story may limp along at first, but relax and soon you will find that it is just unfolding by itself. You may be surprised at the turns the story takes, events that you hadn't even considered.

Here is an example from one of my groups. This woman chose the words seed, fire, father, crocodile, and goblin and wrote the following tale in twenty minutes during a group exercise.

> Once upon a time in a far distant land there lived an ugly green goblin. He was a happy goblin, content with his simple life. When he looked out from his

cave each morning, dewdrops falling from over-
hanging brambles and vines would caress his face. He
would smile from within and breathe deeply and give
thanks for the new day. Life was good.

Increasingly, however, a yawning loneliness was
becoming apparent. On this day he decided to go deep
into the forest, farther than he had ever been, to find
some answers to his longing. He took with him his
good-luck piece, a soft, round tamarind seed that his
father had given him before he had left on his final
journey into spirit. He loved the seed very much. It
was, in a way, his closest friend.

Deep in the forest the goblin encountered a
menacing crocodile that breathed fire. The goblin
held tightly to his tamarind seed for strength. He had
never seen anything so ugly or so menacing before.
Instinctively he wanted to run away, but something
stopped him. The tamarind seed lept from his hands to
the ground between him and the crocodile.

From within, a beautiful light emerged that
encompassed them both; looking through the light to
the crocodile, the goblin saw a new image of a joyous,
loving being staring back from within the green
crocodile skin. The crocodile too saw a joyous friend
staring back from within the fleshy baggage of the
ugly goblin. Now, moving with love, no longer
needing strength nor courage from his tamarind seed,
the goblin rushed to meet his new friend, the
crocodile. The crocodile, with the same realization,
moved quickly to his new companion for life.

As the woman shared this with the group, she felt stunned
and moved to tears by the power of her tale and by the richness of
the imagination that lay within her. In many ways this tale
touches upon some of the powerful forces at work in grief. The
goblin is stirred out of his known world by a yawning loneliness,
just as a grieving person is stirred out of his or her known world.
In the darkness of the forest, he undergoes a great trial, the
terrifying encounter with the crocodile, just as in the dark passage of grief we often come face to face with frightening forces
and realizations.

The goblin's choice to stay and confront the crocodile leads to his transformation; he sees what had threatened him in a new light, his heart opening to love and the joy of companionship. In *Letters to a Young Poet* the poet Rilke writes of dragons, rather than crocodiles, in the same context: "Perhaps the dragons of our lives are princesses who are only waiting to see us once beautiful and brave" (p. 69). Likewise, through our meeting with the dragons of grief, we can be transformed; we see life through different eyes.

In working with these exercises you will be accessing the imaginative powers that are needed to perceive another reality. As I have said before, at first you may feel disappointed as you wander about unable to see or experience anything. Gradually the images will come, but then it is very likely you will discredit them, question their validity, and wonder, Am I making this up?

I have observed that many struggle with or even block the flow of their imagination because they are constantly interfering with and judging the images that present themselves. When we are confronted with an image that we don't understand, our critical mind is often all too ready to interfere, analyzing and judging the image to death. These images ask to be respected and accepted as they are. Then they retain the power invested in them to move and inspire us, even when we don't understand them at all.

One of my clients sat for weeks with an image of a rock crushing a tender flower, which had come to her spontaneously during a short meditation in our session together. This image moved her to tears, although she had no understanding of what it meant. Daily she spent a few minutes just sitting and watching this flower in her mind's eye, letting it be however it presented itself that day.

Then, suddenly, one day the insight came to her that she had felt very much like the little flower as a child, suffering under the weight of crushing, rocklike parental forces. Every time she tried to expand or try something new, her parents put her down and crushed her enthusiasm.

By the time she had this insight, the image was changing dramatically, as though the image were leading the way, a few steps ahead of her understanding of it. The flower was growing. The rock rested at the base, supporting the flower's growth by gathering the warmth of the sun and conserving moisture in the soil. As she nurtured her inner life and dealt with the oppressive forces in her life, the flower grew into a large plant. She still uses this image to check on the state of her psyche.

The following exercise will help you to develop a nonjudgmental, nonanalytical, receptive awareness that has respect and reverence for the power of the images that present themselves to you in your imagination:

Sit comfortably and clear your mind, letting the thoughts drift across the sky of your mind like clouds. Focus on that empty blue sky until an image appears—it can be anything. Be aware of any tendency to judge it, to push it aside because it isn't exciting enough or because it is too ugly or too ordinary. Receive that first image and focus your full attention on it for a few minutes, just letting it be. Let the image work on you in its own way. It may change as you watch it; it may stay the same.

Watch for any desire to interfere, to control the image, to make it what you want it to be. Trust it. Perhaps you may want to come back to this image daily, taking a few minutes at a time to focus upon the image and let it be or unfold as it will.

CHAPTER 10

Bridging the Worlds

Now you are ready to embark on a shamanic journey. The journey will give you a structure that has been used for thousands of years in all parts of the world for entering and exploring this invisible world. It will become a resource you can return to again and again throughout your grief for guidance, comfort, strength, new perspectives, and healing. The journeys will guide you through each stage and every crisis. They will open your vision beyond old limiting structures and beliefs to other realities brimming with possibilities. Death and loss will take on new meanings.

Prepare your sanctuary for your journey, setting aside at least an hour. It is very important that you not be disturbed, for you will be traveling into other realities, and a sudden disturbance in the room could be very disorienting.

Some people like to devote some time before the journey to drumming, singing, lighting a candle, praying, burning incense, or smudging themselves with sage as purification. These activities help in making the transition from everyday reality.

Drumming is like the horse that carries one through the journey. You should use a tape of drumming, half an hour in length, if you are alone. You can either prepare your own or send for one that Michael Harner has prepared for this purpose. In a group you can use a tape if everyone wants to journey; however, it is a special treat when a friend volunteers to drum for the journey, the vibrations resonating throughout the body.

When you have made the transition to the sacred time and space, lie down and cover your eyes, as it is important to journey in darkness. Search your memory for a hole that you have seen in this reality—it can be a gopher hole, cave, spring, well, or tree trunk, or any hole that you feel comfortable with. It is important, however, that you not be able to see the end of it. Your task on the first journey is to become acquainted with passing through this hole and along a tunnel to the entrance to the other world. This tunnel is very similar to the long, dark passage of the second stage of grief; both serve as transitions between the worlds.

Many people spend their first journey struggling with getting down the hole and passing along the tunnel. Fears of the unknown or obstructions in the tunnel may get in the way. Persistence is the key; I have observed many who struggled in their first journeys rewarded with rich ones later. Others are able in their first journey to make their way to the entrance of the other world.

As it is important to have guidance and protection in exploring this other world, the next task is to find your power animal. There is a power in the animal world, recognized by many cultures but for the most part ignored by our own. Through this animal guardian, you can once again connect with the power of the animal world. Often this animal has already sought your attention, perhaps through nightmares as a child, in an unusual encounter, or in repeated pictures that you come across. A woman in a workshop I led took a journey to meet a power animal. But when a giant cobra rose up in her face, she willed the image away, wanting something more cuddly. As we explored this further, she shared that she had had nightmares about snakes as a child, the snake thus calling for her attention. Often the power animal will first present itself in a frightening manner, almost as though it were testing us. It probably will be a momentous turning point in this woman's life when she can accept the power and guidance of this snake.

It is also possible to metamorphose into your power animal. Suddenly you may be flying as a great bird, slithering through the grass as a snake, or stalking prey through the jungle as a leopard.

Once you have connected with your power animal, you can

begin to explore this other world. This world is divided into three levels connected by a central axis. You can travel to the Lower World, often the area of first exploration. Moving down the tunnel or a series of tunnels or passages into the earth, you will come into contact with your power animal. Much healing takes place in the Lower World.

To reach the Upper World one must find a starting point from which one can rise up—perhaps a chimney, whirlwind, tree, or pole. The latter two often serve as the central axis of the three levels. Just as with the Lower World, there are many levels that one can pass through, each level different. One travels to the Upper World, the home of the ancestors, to bring down information, power, and healing. Many meet their teachers there.

The Middle World is reached in a horizontal direction, and many of the places there are similar to places we know in ordinary reality. My Middle World journeys have taken me to hospitals, my parents' house, Armenia after the earthquake, and Alaska after the oil spill.

It is important that you move into this invisible world with some purpose—a question, perhaps, or the intention of healing yourself or another. Exploring this world just to experience it is not enough. The information and power must be brought back to this reality to help and serve others. I feel that my own journeys progressed so rapidly because I was journeying for a clear purpose, for my father's healing into death and for my own preparation for his dying.

Each journey can last half an hour or more. At the end of the journey the drums change rhythm and then pick up pace. This is a signal that it is time to leave whatever you are doing and move back up the tunnel and through the hole into ordinary reality. At that point you can open your eyes. It is helpful to reflect a few minutes on the journey while the images are still fresh. I take this time to write down notes about the journey and to savor the power of the images.

It may take a while for the inner faculties of perception to adjust themselves. During this period of adjustment, you may wander in the invisible world unable to see or imagine. With persistence, this new world begins to reveal itself through the imagination. At this stage it is common to question your experience, "Is this real? Am I making this up?" This demonstrates our lack of trust in the imagination. One woman in a group I led closed her eyes tightly as she emerged from the tunnel in her journey, afraid that she would make up what she had experienced in that world.

As the journeys progress, the imaginal body not only moves without conscious intention but often moves into images alien to the ego. Accustomed to seeing the world from one perspective and determining its version of reality, the ego is jolted and threatened at first by these experiences.

It is disconcerting to fly or change shape and form, defying the laws of ordinary reality. In one workshop, a woman, lying on the floor with her eyes closed, was deftly changing into different animals, reveling in the dolphin's watery play, feeling the power of a tiger crouching on hot rocks, digging in the dark, damp earth as a gopher. Then I directed the group to fly as eagles, transforming into their human bodies as they flew.

Suddenly this woman, who had only moments before soared ecstatically as an eagle in flight, panicked as she saw her human form grasping at the air. "I can't fly." When she shared her experience, she realized that her concepts from ordinary reality had interfered with the limitless possibilities inherent in the imaginal world.

However, with repeated journeys the ego becomes more fluid and flexible, able to experience situations from different perspectives. This is essential in order to fully experience this other world, for there, anything is possible. As the ego is transformed, images and events of the invisible world occur spontaneously without the interference of the judging mind. This paves the way for experiencing the mysteries and surprises of this other world. With each visit, you will grow more accustomed to new perspectives, meet new guides and companions, and learn the geography of inner landscapes. At some point you will feel that you are no longer traveling to a foreign land but returning home. Then you will be living in two worlds.

CHAPTER 11

Initiation

When I next visited Dad, I became aware of a gentle shift within myself. I felt more at peace with him. I wasn't fighting the way he was dying. On this particular day, we had a quiet family lunch together and then he retired to the bedroom to rest. I sat with him there, talking and holding his hand. He expressed no fears about the cancer, only discomfort with the pain. I could tell that the pain was far greater than he would show and knew that he was thinking and feeling things he couldn't share. While I admired his courage, my heart hurt for him.

To my surprise he drew a small crystal out of his pocket; this was his way of telling me that he was now open to alternative healing. He asked that I do some energy work on him. I will never forget the sweetness of those moments standing over him as I worked, looking down on his face, which was so vulnerable and pale. For a few fleeting minutes I held my breath as a waxen, lifeless shadow fell across his face. I could feel that death wasn't far away. It was already tapping on his shoulder, beckoning him home.

Dad, like most of us, had not been prepared for death in life. He seemed to feel that death was a defeat rather than a culmination of one's life, those final moments an opportunity to recognize one's true nature. As I looked at my father's face, I was reminded of my grandfather's face after he died.

Ten years before, I had awakened one morning with the absolute conviction that I had to drive to Marin County to see my grandfather. For weeks he had been in a coma, unattached to life-support systems; my grandmother clung to the bed, crying. When my parents called me about the situation, I suggested that my grandfather was not able to die because of her unwillingness to let him go. My parents talked to her and she finally said good-bye to him.

That was the day I felt so strongly pulled to go to the hospital. I did not hesitate as I had years ago with Dr. Joshi, one of my professors in college. In his class, Dr. Joshi first introduced me to Eastern religion, invoking wonder and surprise in me as we read ancient texts and explored their applications in different practices. Many years later, after meditation had become a central focus of my life, quite out of the blue I started thinking of him and felt moved to call him to thank him for his inspiration. I procrastinated for several days, in spite of the inner prompting I felt to call him immediately. Finally, when I did call him, I was told that he had died the day before.

This time I trusted that inner prompting. I arrived half an hour after my grandfather's death; the rest of the family had left the hospital. Grandfather's shrunken body stretched out on the hospital bed had been vacated; the room, however, was humming with energy.

I immediately knew in my heart that my grandfather had called upon me to support him in this transition; I felt deeply honored to be present at this most precious and critical time after his death. As I have understood from my own experiences in meditation, and from reading *The Tibetan Book of the Dead* as well as accounts of near-death experiences compiled by Elisabeth Kübler-Ross, Raymond Moody, and Kenneth Ring, dying is a process that continues for some time after the vital signs cease. During that time there is an expansion beyond the limited form of the body and an encounter with a light of overwhelming brilliance. One can recognize this as the light of our true nature and merge with it; apparently many miss this opportunity for liberation, experiencing instead many changing images projected by the mind as it runs through its old conditioning.

Jon and I sat next to my grandfather's body. I touched his hand—it was cold and stiff. His face had a white pallor. I put my hand on the top of his head—this was warm and vibrating with energy. I had been told that the life force often leaves the body through the top of the head. We closed our eyes and meditated, sending him love and urging him to let go into the light. I could sense his ambivalence about leaving my grandmother; she was very frightened and lonely without him. Gradually over the next hour the tangible presence of energy in the room seemed to dissipate and then depart. There was a sense of great peace, of completion.

These images of my grandfather dissipated as I looked down at my father on the bed. My breath caught in my throat as I realized that this face as well would soon be only a memory. Death was moving closer; my own parent was dying. I was next in line. No more buffer, no more pretending.

Dad was looking up at me, waiting for me to work on him. I felt a power surge through me; my hands took on a life of their own and started to dance over his body. My hands never touched him but worked with energy fields around his body in intricate, graceful patterns.

Whenever I am doing this energy work, my hands feel the variations of intensity, pressures, and rhythms of each person's energy field. I am struck with how joyful, spacious, and light that energy is when it is flowing and how heavy, cramped, and dark it is when it is not. The energy dancing through my hands seems to lovingly coax and stimulate the person's own energy to lighten and flow again, awakening the innate wisdom of the body to heal itself. The physical body mirrors any obstruction in flow taking place in the person, whether emotional, mental, or spiritual— perhaps static or rigid mental concepts, unexpressed feelings, resistance to impending changes, adherence to outgrown doctrines or beliefs.

As I worked on Dad that afternoon, I noticed that my hands were drawn to his upper abdomen. The energy there was dark and compressed. This felt like some focal point of his illness. I concentrated on that area until the energy began to lighten. I could see that Dad was relaxing, and then his snores signaled sleep. He was no longer in pain.

•   •   •

I continued going on my inner journeys; daily I was prepared for each successive stage of my father's illness and of my own grieving. I experienced a profound healing, emerging often from the journeys with the resources, understanding, and power with which to deal with the daily crises.

As I became more comfortable in taking the journeys, their intensity seemed to increase. Soon I was subjected to initiation rituals—my body was cut open, skinned, slashed, burned. I was locked in a coffin and left lying in the darkness. I often came back from these journeys crying, in a sweat, shaken. As horrible as these experiences were, I felt a strange comfort in such a tangible expression of what I had been feeling emotionally for weeks.

Mircea Eliade has written a great deal about initiation in his book *Rites and Symbols of Initiation,* expressing his concern that modern society is devoid of the meaningful rites of initiation that have been a part of all ancient cultures. For the most part, initiation must now take place inwardly in one's dreams or ecstatic experiences, without the external supports of the culture.

Eliade describes the basic pattern of all initiations: first, the torture at the hands of spirits; second, the ritual death; third, the resurrection to a new mode of being. Through initiation we die to what we were; we do not emerge from these ordeals as the same person. As Plato said, "To die is to be initiated."

In his second session with me, a client described the following dream, which he had had a few days after our first session: he lay on an operating table and without anesthesia was being sliced open down the middle of his body. He watched as his organs were removed one by one to be replaced by new ones. This man had had no exposure to any knowledge of shamanic practices, and yet this clearly was a ritual that many shamans describe in their initiations. The dream suggested to me that the therapy would be a major transformative experience for him, that he was ripe for a psychic initiation and rebirth.

My next journey led me through a vivid initiation ritual involving the sun, similar to the Wiwanyag Wachipi of the Sioux Indians, which means "dance looking at the sun."

The wolf greets me at the mouth of the tunnel, telepathically communicating to me that today I am to be further prepared for the sun ceremony. He leads me up a mountain to a cave. After crawling along a tunnel in darkness, we climb up a central shaft, emerging on a hot, barren plateau at the top of the mountain.

An eagle flies down and lands before me. With wings still spread, it seems to tower over me. I begin to step back, only to be pinned by its penetrating eyes. It orders me: "Remove your clothes and lie naked in the sun." My hesitation is greeted by a simple word that reverberates throughout the plateau: "Now."

I scramble to pull off my clothes and lie down on the warm, crusty earth. After only a few minutes of the blazing sun, I am uncomfortably hot and my skin is blistering. I want to get up and walk away, but the eagle still hovers over me, watching my every move and, I am now convinced, my every thought as well. Its screeching voice jars my body; my thoughts evaporate like popping bubbles. "Look directly into the sun. And do not look away."

Doing this, I am flooded with a light so bright that my eyes can no longer see. Burning light blazing everywhere. I can't even feel my body anymore. Dazzling light. I pass out from the intensity.

All at once I am the eagle soaring toward the sun, flying straight toward its center. As I near it, a strong, white wind pulls me in, until I am engulfed by bright light, brilliance beyond words. I sense the presence of a being of light nearby; I cannot see it, for my normal senses do not seem to function. This being tells me that this light is within all beings, but many do not recognize it until the moment of their death. I must not be afraid to shine fully. Then I see myself standing naked, arms outstretched in a joyous gesture, enveloped in light. I feel new, like a baby.

A shift and I am the eagle again, flying back to the mountain. As I land beside the naked body lying stretched

out in the middle of the plateau, I notice her eyes
beginning to flutter open. I awaken in my human body,
disoriented and exhausted. Unable to move, I look around
me. The colors are so vivid and vibrant: blue sky
overhead, an eagle circling in the distance. The plateau
stretches on all sides in a swath of golden brown.

Tears brim as my eyes finally come to rest on the
silvery snout of my friend and guide, the wolf. In his
presence, I feel my body gaining strength again and I sit
up. He nuzzles me softly, as though to prepare me for
what we are to do next. He tells me we are to dive into
the hole at the center of this plateau. He nuzzles me again,
softening the resistance that I immediately feel welling up
in me.

The wolf takes a few steps toward the hole and then
disappears. Knowing that I must follow, I creep to the
edge of the hole and look down into darkness, a silent
void of black. I take a breath to summon courage and
dive, falling a long way in total darkness.

Finally, the wolf and I are standing in a subterranean
cavern, a pool of water before us. On the shore is a long
boat, filled with twelve hooded figures. They beckon me
wordlessly to join them in the boat, and we float through
tunnels to a cavern where crystals cover the walls in a
mantle of sparkling light. These crystals are called record
keepers and are encoded with ancient knowledge.

The twelve gesture for me to lie down on a large stone
in the middle of the floor. As I do, a large crystal rises out
of the earth to cradle my head. One of the twelve places
crystals between my eyes and on my solar plexus,
massaging them on my skin, creating strange sensations
there. Suddenly I see sparks of light leaping from crystal
to crystal in rainbow arcs across the cavern. I am told that
as each crystal gains some new awareness, another crystal
immediately receives it; this transmission is seen as sparks
of rainbow light. I watch this wondrous display. Then the
hooded figure gently stands me up and tells me it is time
to go back. Just then the drums signal for me to return.

For a long time following this journey, I lay resting, knowing
that I had received much more than I had words to express.

CHAPTER 12

New Perspectives

The dying and death of a parent trigger a process of initiation, sometimes one that is long overdue. In the basic pattern that applies to all initiations, we feel tortured. We die over and over again as we have to let go of old beliefs, structures, and ways of being. We die to who we were.

In ancient cultures, initiation was incorporated into the very fabric of life, rituals marking each major life transition. Our culture, on the other hand, is seriously lacking in the rituals that could help us with these transitions. For example, each family struggles with separation issues as a child matures into adulthood; often separation is not fully and cleanly achieved. The death of a parent can bring to the surface all the unresolved separation issues, thereby complicating the grief.

Other cultures, both past and present, have acknowledged the importance of marking with ritual the transition from childhood to adulthood. This took different forms in different cultures. In his video, "A Gathering of Men," Robert Bly describes a ritual still practiced today in New Guinea. The boy who is considered ready for initiation into manhood undergoes a ritual enactment of separation. Armed with spears, he and his mother walk onto a bridge. They are met by a group of men, also armed, who threaten to take the boy. The boy clings to his mother, looking to her to protect him as she always has.

But this time it is different. He knows that a major change is about to take place, and like all of us he clings to the comfort of the known until he is wrenched away. The time for separation has come, and after a long mock battle the boy is led by the men away from his mother. It is a poignant moment, for there is no going back. He is leaving his old life.

They take him to an island where he will live isolated from the rest of the community, struggling to assimilate new perspectives in preparation for his return. After weeks or months he emerges as a man with a new name and place in the community. He has died as a boy and been reborn as a man.

This initiation ritual can serve as a metaphor for what we pass through when a parent dies. On a bridge between two worlds, the known one behind and the unknown one before us, we desperately make a stand against the forces that threaten to change our life as we had known it. We know deep down what is to follow, but something in us wants to fight the inevitability of death, of loss, of aging. We look perhaps to our parents to protect us, but they cannot, will not. We feel alone and afraid, yet strangely excited about the coming changes. Finally the battle is over—perhaps we have finally accepted our fate or we have been overcome by stronger forces than we can fight.

Then we are led into the territory of grief, where nothing is certain or predictable. And what happens on the island while we are separated from the rest of the community? In that dark time of isolation we begin to question, searching for new meanings and ways of being.

The death of a parent, in true initiatory fashion, shakes up the very foundations of our lives. Daily routines are disrupted, assumptions about life and death jolted, values challenged. The gut-wrenching awareness of our own mortality, of the fragility of life, of the depth and intensity of our feelings, of the power of love and the reality of our aloneness thrusts us into a relentless and often painful questioning that probes to the depths of things, searching for meaning. We may ask, "What is the purpose of my life? What is death? What do I really value? Is there a God? What is God? Does my life really matter?"

There are not many times when we are willing to subject our lives to this scrutiny, for it is painful and unsettling. It takes courage to acknowledge that there is emptiness in our daily lives, that we have compromised our aliveness for security, that our existence has become mechanical and dead. It takes courage to question why we are here, our beliefs about God, our relationship to the universe.

If you want to emerge transformed from the long, dark passage of grief, it is critical at this time to question, probe, and inquire into your life. There may not be ready answers to alleviate your anxiety; at times you may stand stunned before the emptiness of your life that has been exposed in your scrutiny. The deeper you probe, the more you may uncover a gnawing dissatisfaction with your work, marriage, relationships, or life-style.

But where the way had seemed blocked and hopeless, you will eventually find new passages, new possibilities. The questioning of what death is, while it may not yield any clear answers, may initiate the beginning of a spiritual path. The struggle with how to live in the face of certain death may lead to a new appreciation of each moment. The disillusionment with your life-style, work, or relationships may spur you on to make changes in these areas.

Many of my clients have made dramatic changes in their lives following the death of a parent. However, I have observed that there is a tendency to avoid the painful period of questioning and examining one's life by jumping headlong into dramatic changes. We may, in our anxiety, grasp at one possibility and in so doing miss others that may be more appropriate. But more important, we may close down the opening to new perspectives that has been initiated by our honest inquiry into life.

During your sanctuary time, take some time to question your values, choices, and life-style, to inquire into death and life. Make a list of the questions that you want to explore, and spend some time with each.

For example, if you were to explore what death is, you might begin by writing down all your present associations with death along with the conditioning about death you learned as a child. You might want to make a list of all the little deaths you have experienced throughout your life. Then be willing to open to new possibilities and information by reading, talking to others, or just sitting with yourself and observing what comes to you out of the silence. You might choose to imagine your own death, experiencing in clear images the circumstances, the people around you, the good-byes, the final moment. Don't expect to come to any final conclusions about death, as your investigation may lead you deeper and deeper into the unknown, into a greater mystery.

As you begin to wrestle with a deeper purpose in life, it is important to acknowledge the dissatisfaction and hurting within. Something deep within you knows that there is something more to life, something about the quality of life, the spirit with which you live. Ask over and over, "Why am I here?" The hurting that this question provokes will take you deeper, through many layers and levels.

On one level you may want to explore your uniqueness. What am I as an individual person here to do? What are the strengths and weaknesses that can serve me? You may begin to contact the force within that guides your unfoldment into a particular kind of person, unique and unprecedented, just as within a seed there is a life force that directs growth into a particular plant, flower, or tree. However, unlike with the plants, often our conscious ideas conflict with that inner urge to become what we are meant to be. Pierre Teilhard de Chardin speaks to this in *The Phenomenon of Man* when he writes, "What is the work of works for man if not to establish in and by each one of us, an absolutely original centre in which the universe reflects itself in a unique and inimitable way?" (p. 261). Still deeper levels of this questioning may lead to exploration of the mysteries of creation and your relationship to God or Spirit.

One way to clarify your values and priorities is to engage in an exercise in which you imagine that you have only six months left to live. How do you want to spend this limited time? Whom do you want to be with? What feels important? What do you want to eliminate from your life? This is a powerful exercise. Many with terminal illnesses have had to undergo this questioning about their lives, which leads often to a new sense of fullness and purpose to their living, even in the face of imminent death.

Our questioning thus supports and deepens the work that the grief has begun of tearing apart old structures, challenging old assumptions and beliefs, and disrupting the patterns we have become accustomed to and often become deadened by. This is a painful process, but growth always seems to involve some pain. Children have growing pains at the times of maximum growth; adolescents certainly experience pain as they grow out of childhood and into adulthood. Even a seed must experience its own version of pain as it pushes through dark soil and cracks open its outer husk, to emerge in a burst of green growth into a vast new world of warm sunlight.

CHAPTER 13

No Resting Place

Just as I was becoming comfortable with this stage of Dad's disease and of my own grieving, a new crisis arose. My mother called with the news that the doctors had decided to put my father in the hospital for intensive chemotherapy. They didn't have any real hope that it would eradicate the cancer, but they thought it would give him a few weeks of relief from pain. I remember thinking, "Help him with the pain! What if the chemotherapy only causes him more suffering?"

In those moments I realized that now my father would be swept up in the arms of the medical establishment, and I was frightened. In my mind's eye I saw battalions of doctors in white coats marching down long, sterile corridors. I could hear the cries of suffering, the moans of the dying. I could see Dad lying alone, a long lump in a narrow metal bed, surrounded by empty walls and machinery, his eyes staring, unresponsive. I wanted to throw off these images. I felt threatened by the looming presence of the hospital, and I wanted desperately to fight it.

I argued with my mother about the wisdom of taking the doctors' advice, but she insisted that there wasn't any other choice. I felt there were certainly other choices. I wanted Dad to be able to die at home, surrounded by his family, in a nurturing environment.

Once he was in the hospital I doubted that he would ever leave. He would be one more sick person, with a plastic identification band wrapped around his wrist. He would be subject to the hospital's laws, routines, and hierarchy of command. And I would have to stand by helplessly, watching him carted off to the basement for radiation, poked with needles, probed with tubes. I would watch him suffer and die in an impersonal and artificial world, another patient for the nurses and doctors, but my dad for me.

However, I was beginning to learn that if I wanted things to happen a certain way, I was bound to be disappointed. Perhaps I would find peace with my father's dying not through the externals happening just right, but through a shift within myself that could accept and embrace whatever might take place.

Once my mother had made her decision, it was clear that the hospital was to be one of the way stations in Dad's journey. I immediately began to prepare myself. I would bring flowers, music, and a statue of St. Francis to make Dad's room more personal. I would surround myself with family and friends for emotional support. I would make a special effort to nurture myself during the hospital visits, a challenge in the face of constant interruptions and stressful procedures, perhaps through meditation, listening to music, or taking walks around the block. Then I would be able to be more fully present with Dad and responsive to the needs of the moment. To tap other resources and perspectives on this situation, I took an inner journey.

I burst through the opening of the tunnel separating ordinary and nonordinary reality, on my feet and running. I arrive at Xan's cave, telling him about the doctor's plan to put Dad in the hospital and administer a chemotherapy solution intravenously for a week.

Xan enters a golden shaft of light to meditate on the situation. When he comes out, he leads me to the crystal cavern, where he joins the eleven shrouded figures. I had discovered in a previous journey that Xan is one of the twelve.

Surrounding Dad in a circle, they lay him on the central stone slab and begin to chant a low, resonant "om." The sound fills the cave and I can feel its power in my body. One of the crystals on the wall emits a flash of rainbow light that penetrates Dad's body; he begins to

*convulse violently. When this ceases, he is smiling, saying,
"I see the angels."*

*Turning to me with love dancing in his eyes, he takes
my hand. We talk together about our relationship, sharing
our love, old resentments and regrets, appreciations. Then
we sit together in silence, absorbing the full impact of the
healing that has just occurred. Xan, standing beside us, is
moved to tears; the rest of the shrouded figures are
enveloped in a reverent hush. Then Dad gently places my
hand in Xan's upturned palms and quietly leaves the cave.*

*Xan guides me to stand beside him in the circle. With
heads bowed and hands extended, the twelve are intently
concentrating. In the middle of the circle they manifest a
living earth in miniature, oceans lapping, forests and
mountains teeming with life. Hands outstretched toward
the earth, they send energy until it is surrounded in golden
radiance. The earth starts to undulate, something pushing
from within, as though it were trying to give birth. But
whatever is within is not ready to emerge yet. The drums
call me back.*

This was the first of many journeys that focused on the
healing and future of the earth. It was perplexing to me why in
the middle of a personal drama of healing, images of healing the
earth should arise as well. Dr. Kenneth Ring has concentrated
recent studies on the prophetic visions of people who have had
near-death experiences. He found that a small number of people
who had undergone a particularly deep near-death experience
had had surprisingly similar visions of the planetary future. As
one person reported in Ring's book *Heading Toward Omega,*
"At the end of this general period of transition, mankind was to
be 'born anew,' with a new sense of his place in the universe. The
birth process, however, as in all the kingdoms, was exquisitely
painful. Mankind would emerge humbled yet educated, peaceful,
and, at last, unified" (p. 198). Ring conjectured that the nearness
of death, whether of the body or ego, could trigger the imagery of
world cataclysm and transformation. My father's dying seemed
to trigger these images as well.

A few days later I had another planetary vision.

I am met by a dolphin in the sea, singing to me in a high-pitched sonic song and brushing me with her silky body. I ride her down to the depths of the ocean, down through passageways of water, deeper and deeper.

Finally we enter a red tube that shoots us straight to the center of the earth. I shrink back from the molten fire that blazes there, the heat burning and melting me. A blacksmith approaches, blackened with layers of soot, his gnarled hands grasping an iron bar; seeing my fear, he assures me that new life is forged in this fire, new life for the earth and for each being that burns in it. As I surrender to the flames I grow hotter and hotter until I am spinning in a pillar of white light.

Abruptly there is an explosion from within this fire that shakes the entire planet, followed by two more explosions. With the fourth explosion, the white light is propelled out into space, exploding into light particles that rain down on earth. As each particle of light lands, a person, animal, plant, or rock is illuminated, creating little fireworks all over the planet. Then whole continents light up, more and more light spreading until the entire earth is a brilliant ball of light. I know that this is the same light that is within me—there is no difference.

I look down at my body and see that my belly is large and round, and mountains, valleys, and rivers are all clearly delineated on it. I am pregnant with the earth. From deep in my uterus, I feel painful contractions and I know that labor has begun. The earth is born between my legs, a small green-blue ball.

I hold her tenderly in my hands, now as Mother Universe. With each movement of my body, planets, stars, trees, birds, animals, people, all life forms appear rippling along the surface of my gown and then disappear into the folds. I hold this precious ball in my hands, appreciating its beauty. This little planet will be a place to explore the coming together of matter and light, of discovering the light in matter. There will be much experimentation and many dangers. I see the atom bomb as one of those dangers, one of the smallest particles of matter exploding into light.

Suddenly, my attention telescopes onto one mountaintop, on which a man is drumming. The drumming is resonating throughout the universe, as

simultaneously the universe resides within that drummer.
A new drumbeat, full and resonant, emerges out of the
steady background beat. The mountain explodes and the
man is propelled into space, dissolving into vast,
shimmering space.

Where the volcano had exploded, I see a huge
opening—the red, pulsing, beating heart of the earth, raw
and vulnerable. This vision is so powerful that I can
barely look upon it.

These images left me so stunned that I could hardly move or talk after the journey. For hours I could feel them silently working within me, thrusting me into boundless space and yet rooting me in the raw and bleeding heart.

Dad entered the hospital, and I knew even then that he would never leave. The tests that were immediately administered showed extensive cancer throughout his bones, liver, and lungs. The cancer had made several large bites into his vertebrae. The doctors could not believe that he had remained active, working right up to the morning he entered the hospital. He was settled in a room two doors down from his previous one, hooked up to the IVs that dripped the chemotherapy solution into his veins around the clock.

Mother stayed at the hospital with Dad, giving me frequent updates by phone. This was a difficult time for her. The events were unfolding so quickly, with each crisis demanding a new decision. She spent hours consulting with Hospice and the doctors at the hospital, trying to maintain mental clarity while she watched her husband disintegrate before her eyes. I admired her ability to cope with these pressures and at the same time keep her heart so open to my father and me.

That day I decided that the time had come to organize a group healing meditation for Dad. I felt strongly that his entrance into the hospital marked a new phase of his illness, perhaps the beginning of the end. A journey of the previous night had allayed my fears about the chemotherapy; I felt that Dad's coming to peace with himself was far more important now.

I started calling friends, asking them to meditate and pray at nine that night, focusing on his healing whether into life or death. I called the New Camaldonian Monastery in Big Sur as well, so that they too would pray for my father. I had attended many retreats there, and I knew the power of their prayers.

More than fifty people meditated and prayed for him that night from their homes all over the country. A small group had gathered at my house as well, sitting around an altar I had set up in the living room arranged with pictures of Dad, a statue of St. Francis, flowers, and candles. By ten minutes after nine the energy was tangibly powerful. As I meditated, an image formed in my mind's eye of Dad being lifted gently by golden beings into a blue expanse.

The next morning, in preparation for my visit to the hospital, I took an inner journey.

A black leopard meets me at the entrance to the tunnel, telling me that he was trying to get my attention last night. I remember that I had awakened suddenly from sleep, startled by the vivid image of a black leopard looking intensely into my eyes. He tells me he wants to help.

He leads me down a series of tunnels, deeper and deeper into the earth. Finally we reach a dark, steamy swamp from which an amorphous mass of muddy substance emerges. This mass tells me in a gravelly voice that it is a guide in murky, oppressive, hopeless situations. It seems to be alluding to the situation with my father and my feelings of helplessness as Dad is pumped full of drugs in the hospital. It directs me to find a mirror under a leaf and take it to my father.

I go and find the mirror, small and oval, cool and hard in my hand. I climb to Belatha's cave, where Dad is staying. Stroking a coyote, she is sitting beside Dad as he rests on the wooden bed. She doesn't know how long she can keep Dad's power animal there, for it wants to leave. I feel a pain in my heart as I remember that in shamanic traditions a person will die soon after a power animal leaves. Saddened, I hand Dad the mirror.

As he looks into it, his life passes before him in a rapid succession of images that flicker across the glass. He

*sees that he is dying. I can sense from his expression that
he recognizes not only the emptiness in what he had so
valued at one time, but also the power of the love he has
given and received, the love he feels for himself.*

*With that awareness, he steps through the mirror to
the other side. There, everything is topsy-turvy, a place of
transition between the worlds where he can finish business
and say good-bye to one world while preparing for
entrance to the other. Belatha tells me that she will stay
with Dad as he explores this place.*

*The leopard takes me to a spring, a stone fount with
steps around it, and tells me, "This is a sacred place of
grieving. The spring will take you deep but bubbles with
resources and new life. Dive into it." I climb up on the
edge of the stone fount and look into its dark waters. I
jump, the cold water shocking my cells awake. Every inch
of my body is tingling.*

*Then I am floating on a simple wooden raft across a
still lake, rocked in my grief as I flow with the tide.
Fairylike creatures bend over me, comforting me. The raft
floats through a luminous archway.*

*I am standing now, full of light, as though I had been
reborn out of my grief and the darkness. The leopard
informs me that through my grief I can learn to love, to
experience the heart of the universe, and to know what is
going on in each heart of that universal heart.*

*I float into a circular cavern; green froglike creatures
are perched all along the rock walls. I pass before each
one and touch its heart, knowing instantly what is going
on within that being. I feel flooded with reverence and
love.*

*I begin to float upward, as though I had been
lightened. Angels cradle me while Jesus stands before me,
radiant, inviting me into his heart. I enter a vibrating
space of exquisite love within which all is contained.
Within that space I see a crucifix of light and know that
when we are crucified in our suffering we can be born into
love. Lights emanate through my arms and legs as I
become a glowing crucifix of light.*

Our wounding opens doors to a sacred space, the violation of
our boundaries wrenching open a window through which larger
forces can enter into our lives. Mythology teaches this: the hero

or the god is wounded, initiating a journey into larger dimensions. Persephone is raped, Osiris dismembered, Zeus's head split open. In shamanic tradition the shaman in training is boiled, cut into little pieces, burned, or flayed in order to make way for a new order. Jean Houston's timely chapter on the Sacred Wound in *The Search for the Beloved* helped me to honor and appreciate my wounding during this period. I wanted to keep the wound open, for it was my window into the vast, unknown, sacred spaces of my psyche.

The next morning Jon and I drove to St. Francis Hospital in San Francisco. I felt comforted that this hospital honored the saint who has been a major source of healing for me. On a trip to Italy with Jon ten years before, I had been drawn to visit the little town of Assisi, the home of St. Francis. After a full day of train travel, Jon and I rode the bus from the train station on the Umbrian plain. My first view of the town nestled up on the hill, its stone buildings aglow in the setting sun, moved me to tears. I had a strange sense of homecoming.

We were soon comfortably ensconced in a room overlooking the tile roofs of the town and the countryside; staying in a convent flooded me with memories of the Catholic schools of my childhood. That evening, in meditation, I was overcome by a stunning sweetness, the likes of which I had never experienced before; I knew this was the spirit of St. Francis. Jon, who does not often have experiences of this nature, also was struck by a sweetness in his meditation.

Indeed, St. Francis's presence is still tangibly felt throughout the town, in the stones, the flowers, the birds. To him the world was a miraculous celebration of God: "All praise be yours, my Lord, through all that you have made." As I wandered down stone alleyways bordered by red geraniums and yielding vistas at every turn, I was moved to celebrate God through my senses. In those days in Assisi, St. Francis taught me to rejoice in God right here on earth; it was to him that I had come to mend the rift between heaven and earth.

We stayed in Assisi over two weeks, feeling unable to leave. I walked to the Hermitage where St. Francis went on retreat, meditating in the cave where he prayed alone. We visited all the churches and monasteries where he lived and died. I was drawn to every aspect of his life, and I read and asked questions about him. Nikos Kazantzakis wrote in his novel *Saint Francis,* "But whenever he spoke, prayed, or thought he was alone, his squat body shot forth flames that reached the heavens. . . . 'Put yourself out, Brother Francis,' I used to cry. 'Put yourself out before you burn up the world' " (pp. 24–25). The volcanic fire of Spirit erupted from the depths of this humble little man, inspiring others for centuries with the vision from this vibrant Source.

As we left Assisi one brilliant morning, I knew that I had established a connection with St. Francis that would inspire, guide, and comfort me for years to come. Upon returning home I was welcomed by a lovely white stone statue of the saint in my garden that seemed to have appeared miraculously during our absence. A client, without any knowledge of my experiences in Assisi, had felt compelled to buy this statue for me and placed it in our garden a few weeks before our arrival.

As we entered the elevator on the way to my father's hospital room, armed with a tape recorder, a small statue of St. Francis, and flowers, I took a deep breath and looked to Jon for support. He smiled at me warmly. I did not know what this visit would bring; the changes were happening so fast.

Dad was lying in bed, cheerfully submitting to the drip, drip of the chemotherapy solution into his veins. We hugged, trying not to get entangled in the tubing. I pulled up the small chair to his bedside, taking his hand. His hand was warm, his cheeks ruddy. So far he exhibited no ill effects except for drowsiness.

We spent the next five hours just sitting together, talking and watching the Crosby golf tournament. He struggled at first to make conversation, but I assured him that we could just sit together. Often he closed his eyes, as though he were seeing into another world. As in my journey, it seemed that he had moved into the transitional space between the worlds.

I wanted to hold him, cry with him, and talk about our relationship, but I was content that the love was flowing between us as we quietly sat together. I felt at peace with Dad loving me in his own way; I finally accepted that Dad and I would just never have the special father-daughter time I had longed for. It was hard to let that dream die, to accept the finality of Dad's impending death.

For so many years I had accepted the nature of our relationship because I had hoped that one day it would change. One day we would spend an afternoon together, just the two of us. One day we would sit down together and talk about our lives, our relationship. It was painful to realize that I had so few memories of time alone with my Dad. Even in family gatherings he would recede to the background behind a *Time* magazine, unwilling to make much contact.

Once in eighteen years I had spent a few hours alone with Dad. He had driven two hours to talk to me about my living with Jon. He had just found out; my mother had felt the need to "protect" him from the truth for a year. He wanted to voice his objections, but he was willing to hear me out. I leaned across the table toward him and said, "Dad, you've always taught me to do whatever I knew was right for me. I know that this is the right thing for me to do." He smiled and responded that he had to respect my choice even though it conflicted with his values. I had cherished that conversation for eighteen years, hoping that again we would connect like that. But the years had gone by. And now I was sitting at his bedside watching him die.

I was quickly initiated into the routine of nurses checking the IV, changing the sheets, and bringing in food. I sat amid the bustle of activity, watching and learning. I felt sad that with all the attention to the machines, so little was given to Dad directly—a comforting touch, a few words of preparation for what to expect next. I could feel the suffering that had gone on in that one room, in that one bed, as person after person had lain there alone hour after hour, dying.

I walked down the ward, looking into the doors of the other rooms. There were so many people suffering, many alone, a few with a relative or friend by their bedside. Most visitors, overwhelmed by the presence of death, didn't stay very long. At the end of the hall, there was a frail Chinese woman talking with her husband. She smiled radiantly at me, a smile that suggested that she knew of the incredible lightness of being even as death hovered over her bed. On my next visit a few days later, this woman's room was empty.

As evening approached, Jon and I decided that it was time to leave, for we needed to pick up Taylor at his friend's where he had been spending the day. As I leaned over to hug Dad, I dissolved into tears, hugging him and telling him I loved him. With each good-bye I was moving closer to the final one.

CHAPTER 14

Saying Good-bye

There comes a time for preparing to say good-bye. Don't rush this; you may not be ready. You may still have unfinished business to take care of with your parent, feelings to express in words, letters, tears.

Throughout a parent's aging or illness there may be opportunities to sit down and clear away the old resentments, share the appreciations and love, and explore the expectations you had of the parent that he or she could not fulfill. These talks can help you come to peace with your parent and in so doing prepare the way for saying good-bye.

Unfinished business can keep us from being able to let go fully and move on with our lives. The old resentments, unfulfilled wishes, and unexpressed love will gnaw, corrode, and sabotage us quietly but insistently. Even when there has been the opportunity in life to share love and resolve old hurts and resentments with one's parent, death often illuminates issues that were kept in the background in life. Perhaps insights into that parent or into the relationship emerge that were too frightening or disturbing to face when the parent was alive.

It is a common experience in grief for many unresolved feelings toward the parent to surface. Many clients have initially expressed a sense of futility, asking, "Why should I do this when it doesn't matter any more? What good will it do now?" But death ends a life, not a relationship. You can work through your unfinished business with your parents without their active participation.

Martina's mother died when she was five years old. No one talked to her about her mother dying; she was not even allowed to go into the room where her body lay. Her father and relatives, with the best of intentions, wanted to protect her, but in so doing they never gave her an opportunity to cry, to mourn, and to heal. Martina was whisked off with her brother to an aunt's house, and life went on as though nothing had happened.

Martina became an achiever, striving to get to the top of her class and then her profession. She ignored the fact that she felt distant emotionally, that she had difficulty being intimate. She learned to go on with her life as though nothing had happened, until at the age of forty she came down with a debilitating illness. With her energy depleted, the coping structures fell apart, releasing many chaotic feelings and memories. She sank into a dark depression.

In our sessions, we explored the stress that the illness was causing in her life; gradually it became evident that the illness was providing her with an opportunity to heal past traumas, one of which was the unresolved grief over her mother's death. The five-year-old in her was given permission to cry, rage, and call out with longing to her mother, "Mommy, where are you? Where have you gone? Why have you left me? I'm so alone without you. Mommy! Mommy!" And the tears began to flow, beginning a journey of healing.

Writing a letter or a series of letters is a very effective means of resolving unfinished business with a parent who is unavailable or who has died. Tell your parent what you are feeling—any resentments, regrets, old hurts, appreciations, love, forgiveness. Explore whatever is unfinished, or unexpressed.

Or you can visualize a meeting with your parent in a nurturing, safe place. This has the added benefit of allowing you to express nonverbally what you are feeling to your parent and to experience your parent's response.

Close your eyes and see him or her standing before you in your mind's eye. Observe closely the expression, body posture, clothes. Be aware of your feelings as you do this. Allow for whatever wants to unfold—perhaps you see yourself interacting with your parent, perhaps your parent leads you somewhere, or perhaps a dialogue develops. Watch and listen carefully, and then record what you have seen and heard.

Now close your eyes again and visualize yourself standing with your parent before a large screen, similar to one you would see at the movies. You are going to witness on this all the stages of your relationship with your parent from birth to the present. Your parent's illness and death become another stage in that continuity, with yet more stages to unfold. Watch closely as the images move across the screen. Perhaps there are periods in which vivid images flood the screen and other periods of sparser images. There may even be blank spaces. Observe your responses to all these images as they scroll past.

As the screen moves up to the present moment and the images cease, evaluate how you are feeling toward your parent. What do you regret, resent, and appreciate in your relationship? Turn to your parent and communicate this. Then open your eyes and record what you have experienced.

———

If you have had difficulty understanding your parent's actions or beliefs in anything you have seen on the screen, you can explore the following exercise:

———

With your eyes closed, summon a clear image of your parent. In your imagination, see yourself move very close to your parent and then step inside. At this point you will be looking at the world through your parent's eyes.

How do you feel? What is your experience of the world? Where have you been wounded? How do you feel as you look at your child before you? Where have you struggled in your relationship? What have you wanted in the relationship? Is there anything you want to communicate to your child?

When you feel complete with this experience, step back outside your parent and observe how you feel in your relationship now. Then open your eyes and record what you have seen and experienced.

———

This exercise has had dramatic results for many clients. One woman suddenly understood the pain that had driven her mother to sacrifice everything for the love of a man, thereby neglecting her young daughter's needs. Sobbing, she touched a place of love for her mother that she hadn't felt since childhood.

Another client, carrying deep resentment toward his alcoholic father who had drunk himself to death, shared that in this exercise he experienced a compassion for his father that he had not felt for years. He realized that his father really did love him. "There was a moment of seeing how my father is proud of me and loves me, a brief glimpse of healing in the morass I feel with him."

I expressed my love and experienced my father's vulnerability in my shamanic journeys in a way that I was never able to do in person. This was tremendously healing to me, opening my heart and giving me the opportunity to live out in the imaginal world the tenderness I had longed for in our relationship. As a result, I felt more at peace with our relationship when he died. Even so, after his death I felt my eyes suddenly opened to aspects of his personality that I had ignored before—I couldn't believe I had been so blind. The love and tenderness I felt for him guided me through the disillusionment to a deeper love that could embrace all of him, not just the parts I wanted to.

Taking care of unfinished business prepares us for the important step of saying good-bye. At first you may resist the finality, wanting to leave the door open, just in case. This culture does little to prepare us for the finality of death—we are taught to acquire and replace, not to let go or lose. We are sheltered from seeing dead bodies. Death is seen as a defeat, not as a natural part of the life cycle. Everything in us wants to hold out for the chance that this has been a mistake, a bad dream. Every so often we catch a glimpse of someone or hear a voice and our heart races— There he is! She is still alive!—but as the months and years pass, the finality penetrates to deeper levels of the psyche, and we begin to accept that our loss is permanent and final.

When you finally accept your loss, you may be ready to say good-bye. This act, often overlooked because it is considered unimportant once the parent has died, helps to bring grief into resolution. It helps you to go on with your life—and your parent to go on. I have seen many clients say good-bye to a parent ten or twenty years after his or her death, and they feel an enormous sense of closure when they do this.

One client's father had died when she was in her teens, shortly after her first act of sexual rebellion. For years after she had disturbing dreams about her father in which he appeared very ill. Early in our sessions it became evident that she had much unresolved grief over his death that was sabotaging her acceptance of her own womanhood. It was as though her sexual development had halted at her father's death, for any exploration had abruptly ceased and her physical changes had slowed dramatically.

As the guilt, sadness, anger, hurt, and forgiveness were explored one by one, the dreams began to shift in nature. Her father became healthy, and then he ceased appearing. In a tearful session she finally was able to say good-bye to him, over thirty years after his death. Many profound changes immediately manifested in her body, her manner of dressing, and her relationships. It was as though her once-frozen sexuality had thawed, and it was now vitalizing her with new energy and passion.

As you say good-bye, you are releasing your parent as you had known him or her. But the love continues, and it may be deeper and fuller as it is freed of the daily personality struggles. I often turn to the well-worn page of Stephen Levine's book *Meetings at the Edge,* to read a woman's letter to her best friend at her mother's death: "Your mother and my mother can never leave us; the temple of their lives may change, but the theme of their vast love, still throbbing in us, will only be continuing somewhere" (p. 90).

CHAPTER 15

The Upside-Down Space

I left the lobby of the St. Francis Hospital in a daze. As I stepped out onto busy Bush Street, I felt vulnerable and raw, unprepared for the onslaught of noise and traffic. Yet even the frenetic activity couldn't distract me from what I felt in my heart. With death so present, what mattered in life was so clear. I was seeing the world through different eyes.

The next day, I visited Belatha in her cave.

Emerging from beneath her red blanket, she throws her arms around me, holding me close to her soft, warm body. When she releases me, I see that Dad is resting on a wooden bed, but his power animal is nowhere to be seen. Responding to my alarm, Belatha tells me, "We must hope that as your father grows weaker physically, he will grow stronger in spirit."

Suddenly, as though in response to Belatha's words, Dad jumps up and starts to dance wildly and exuberantly. I am taken aback by this sudden change, but then I realize that he is dancing his life. I watch intently as his movements flow from one into another, full of feeling and passion. Then he slumps down, exhausted. Belatha tells me that it is time for me to leave.

This journey seemed to signify further work in that place of transition between the worlds. I was very moved by the vision of Dad dancing his life. I could savor the expression of all the different stages and events of his life as his body moved them.

The next journey suggested that Dad was moving closer to death.

A thick, green snake appears after I come out of the tunnel. I ignore it, hoping for another guide, but it entwines itself around my legs and arms, forcing me to acknowledge its presence. Then it slides down a hole, beckoning me to follow. We go down many levels, each level progressively darker.

Finally, two beams of light penetrate the total darkness, and I realize as they move closer that they are the eyes of some imposing being. The being tells me telepathically, "I am the guardian of death. I guide people at this powerful time."

I ask about my father. He replies, "Death is a change to another level. Your father resisted making that change in life, and so now he will make it in death. All that resistance caused the pain he is experiencing now, for he has obstructed a natural flow. The pain is breaking down that obstruction."

I ask him to show me what Dad will experience at his death. He points to his black cloak, which I can barely distinguish from the darkness: "This is only the surface layer of death." Then he pulls it aside, revealing a radiant light sparkling from within. It is as though within this simple cloak, a dazzling sun or shining star throbbed in seclusion, eager to burst its tentative boundaries and cast its radiance throughout the universe. The vision is breathtaking.

I stumble away, the snake following close behind. It begins to wrap around my body playfully. When it suddenly bites my arm, I am shocked and hurt. The snake tells me that I must cry, for otherwise I too will be obstructing a flow.

Still feeling upset by this treatment, I leave and search for one of my teachers. I find Mikael in an archway of clouds, his transparent body barely distinguishable from the surrounding sky. He says, "Stand in the wind and let it blow through you. Let the feelings flow through you, moment by moment, like the wind blowing through you. You must not hold on even to grief. Remember this whenever you feel the wind."

*His words stir something deep in me, and I begin to
cry, my body convulsing with sobs. Mikael tenderly
holds me.*

Ever since that journey I have experienced the wind in a new
way. Whether it is a gentle breeze or a strong, gusty wind, I have
let it blow through my body, pouring through every pore of my
skin and through every cell of my body. When the grief comes,
my body remembers to let it flow through without obstruction.

Between visits with my father, I welcomed the rhythm of
daily life, my commitments as a mother and as a therapist
grounding me, reminding me that life goes on in the presence of
death. As the days passed, I often thought back on an event that
had occurred within minutes after hearing the message on my
answering machine that Dad had cancer. That day a client had
called to tell me that her baby had just been born. Even in that
moment of shock and grief, I had felt the excitement and wonder
of birth and had shared the mother's joy. This juxtaposition
of life and death continued to have a profound effect on me, reminding me of the larger picture. Just as life passes away, so new
life arises.

During this time, client after client came to me struggling to
deal with the death or dying of a parent. For some, the wounds of
a death long ago still bled. It seems that my therapy practice
consistently mirrors the concerns, rhythms, and developments of
my inner life, and this time in my life was no exception. If I have
recently made a discovery in myself, clients will present problems
that challenge me to consolidate and share these insights. Any
unresolved issue within me inevitably draws clients who bring
me face to face with it. With each new level of consciousness I
attain, clients appear ready to engage me on that level. Even my
client schedule seems to swell and shrink in harmony with some
inner rhythm of expansion and withdrawal. I am continually
awed by and grateful for the opportunity to participate in this
mutual dance of transformation.

Before my next visit to the hospital, I went on an inner

journey in which my guide sat down with me and imparted some important instructions:

> "*The period your father is now entering will have a crazy upside-down quality. Let others take care of your father's body. Your work is to care for his spirit, guiding it toward the light. His soul will appear as a ball of light, merging into a greater light. You will know when he has made his passage.*"
>
> *The last statement hits me with a jolt, as I realize that I may not be with my father when he dies; I feel very sad and disappointed. Sensing my sadness, Xan takes my hand and holds it lovingly in his. I begin to cry for joy, for I know in that moment that even as I am losing a father in one world, I am gaining one in another. I feel tremendous comfort in knowing that this father is so accessible in my inner world.*
>
> *Xan stands and leads me to the crystal cavern. The twelve surround me, chanting a simple chant, flowing energy toward me through their outstretched hands. The crystals on the stone walls light up, shooting arches of rainbow light from one side of the cave to the other, each beam passing through my body in its transit. I look up and see a beautiful star in the center of the domed ceiling. Transfixed and stunned by its power, I stand motionless for a long time, drinking in this exquisite vision, as though I had come to a spring of healing waters after a long drought. After a long time, Xan softly touches my arm to get my attention, saying, "This is your star, to guide and inspire you on your journey through life. Allow it to speak to you in its own way. You have much to learn from it." I weep, overcome with reverence and awe, my heart feeling a strong sense of homecoming.*
>
> *When I stand to go, I feel strong in body and spirit. I share my gratitude and leave for the hospital to visit Dad. His power animal, the coyote, is there, lying in a corner of the room. I pet her gently and then turn to Dad, stroking his head and telling him that I love him.*
>
> *Then I am standing in a clearing in the woods, animals gathering around me: wolves, birds, coyote, deer, mountain lions, gophers, rabbits. They seem to be telling*

*me that nature will comfort me in my grief. As I lie down
on the earth, tiny flowers burst into bloom, creating a
carpet of purple velvet. I watch them stretching with
determination toward the light, tottering on the tips of
slender stems. I am inspired by their quiet persistence in
fulfilling a cycle, no matter how short the season. A fawn
appears, gentle and new, its liquid brown eyes meeting
mine.*

That afternoon my mother called with the news that Dad's
lungs were filling with fluid. He was restless but not in pain,
struggling to move his weakened body off the bed to go to the
"ball game." I knew that this was the crazy upside-down space
that I had seen in my journey. I made arrangements to go to the
hospital for an extended visit.

Early Friday morning we packed and drove Taylor to Jon's
parents' house. Jon and I had asked Taylor if he wanted to come
to the hospital with us, preparing him for some of the changes
that he could expect: "Granddad is in bed all the time now; he is
too weak and sick to get up. He's going to look much different
than he did the last time you saw him." He had thought carefully
and then said, "No. I think it would be too sad." I respected the
boundaries he needed to set for himself.

We had shared with Taylor from the beginning that his
granddad was sick with cancer, that he was dying. We had talked
about death, exploring together the questions, concerns, and
feelings that arose. His last experience with death had been a
positive one; he often shared with us his memories of his cat's
death and burial, explaining to us that his cat was no longer in
the body in the ground under the oak tree, for his spirit was now
everywhere.

As my father was dying, Taylor became aware of the fact that
his parents would die someday, too. His main concern was that
he not be left behind, so he often asked me if I would die before
him. I told him that I didn't know when I would die but that it
was very possible that I wouldn't die until he was an adult. I
pointed out that my dad was dying and I was okay. My tears
were not from regret that death had come to him, for this was a

natural process, and it was Granddad's time to die. I cried because I would miss Dad in his body form.

Taylor could see that Dad's dying did not weigh me down, that there were times when I felt light and happy as well as times when I felt sad or pensive. He was very interested in my meditations and journeys for Dad; he listened with rapt attention when I shared one with him. One day he asked, "Mama, when I die will you pray for me as many hours as you pray for Granddaddy?"

Taylor was processing all this information, learning about death's place in life, watching me carefully for cues. I knew that how I was dealing with Dad's dying had a profound effect on his own attitude toward death. His comments, so fresh and clear, gave me clues as to how he was integrating all this. One day he hugged me when I was crying and sweetly said, "Why are you crying so hard? You know that Granddaddy's spirit will always be with you!"

When Jon and I walked into the hospital room, I was shocked at the changes in Dad in only a week. His eyes were glazed, unseeing, his body limp, his breathing raspy. Mother had been at his side hours a day for the past week, and she was exhausted, resting at home. I sat down next to him, stroking him tenderly, holding his hand.

From time to time he rose out of the delirium and saw me sitting at his side. He would squeeze my hand, a sweet smile of recognition lighting his features. Then his eyes would glaze over again as he retreated into his inner world.

Jon and I stayed all day, returning after a short dinner break to meditate in the room. Silently I talked to Dad through my heart, guiding him into the light. The hours passed quickly, and soon it was late, time to get some sleep. I was tired and yet reluctant to leave.

I had begun to see a pattern in my hospital visits—no matter how refreshed I felt when I entered the hospital, I was exhausted within an hour. I would have expected time to drag, but it didn't. The hours disappeared quickly, and all too soon it was time to leave again. I didn't like leaving once I was there. I wanted to be there with Dad.

As Jon and I drove to my parents' house, I was jolted by the recognition that Dad would never return here. How suddenly life could change! In his bathroom, his vitamins and medications were lined up carefully, a *Time* magazine was rolled to one side, and his leather slippers rested next to the half-full laundry basket, a poignant expression of his daily routine, to which he would now never return.

I crawled into bed, every muscle in my body aching. I slept fitfully, waking often with the image of Dad lying alone in the hospital room. In the middle of the night I was jolted awake by a vision of Dad standing in the doorway, yellow light all around him. He spoke to me: "I've come to say good-bye. Take care of Mother. I'm okay. I'm with Jesus." The vision was so clear and powerful that I expected any moment to hear the phone ringing with the news that Dad had died. But no call came, and I drifted off to sleep again as the birds started to sing outside the window.

Upon awakening, Jon and I hurried back to the hospital. Expecting to see Dad on his deathbed, I took a big breath and stepped quietly into his room. With a shock I beheld an empty bed. Dad was sitting in a chair, his naked legs stretched out before him in the warm sunlight. He looked up from his conversation with his friend, Jerry Jampolsky, and greeted us warmly. I felt a great happiness well up in me as I hugged him, feeling him so present with me. It was as though he had returned from another world.

All day my father received his friends and family, sharing stories and jokes. He had wanted no one to know he was in the hospital, but on this one day many of his close friends came to visit and to share their love. There was no mention of his dying, but he spoke his heart with each person.

Dad was saying good-bye, just as he had said good-bye to me the previous night; he had been granted this last burst of energy for this purpose. He was dying as he had lived—with courage and dignity. The hall was filled with friends weeping, many stricken with the recognition that death could come so suddenly to someone they had considered invincible. Dad had done such a good job at hiding his illness that most of his friends were unprepared.

Toward the end of the afternoon, Dad was no longer in the hospital in his mind. He was living in Hawaii in the days of his courtship with my mother, one of the most magical and happy times of his life. He told us all to get dressed for the party, musing about the food that would be at the luau. He used the Hawaiian names for these delicacies, words I hadn't heard since I was a child. Then he looked at the picture on the wall, a painting of a field of flowers, and commented on the three battleships depicted there.

By that evening the pain had returned and he sank back into the bed, exhausted. He had completed his farewells. I sat with him into the night as he slept, meditating and talking to him through my heart.

The next day he was comatose. His eyes glazed over, he lay looking into another world; he was so soft and vulnerable, like a newborn, each breath growing shorter and the spaces between them longer. His heartbeat became very irregular. It seemed he was dying. Only once did he come out of the coma to tell us that he loved us. We were gathered around his bed—Mother, Jon, Taylor, and I.

That morning Taylor had expressed his desire to see Grand-daddy. His immediate reaction as he walked into the hospital room was shock. "Why does he look so old?" He took it all in, the sound of raspy breathing, Dad's half-open, unseeing eyes, the IV tubes. He realized that we were comfortable with all this, and within moments he had settled into active acceptance of the scene. He asked me, "Can I talk to Granddad?" I explained to him that he could, that people in comas can often hear while they cannot respond.

Taylor proceeded to tell Granddad all about his day. His vitality filled the sterile room, life overflowing in the presence of death. He questioned the nurses about the machines and IVs; he was fascinated by the little bubbles of air that flowed through the tubes. When Jon took him out for a while, I meditated with Dad, guiding him into the light, holding the hand I'd held so many times, feeling the love pulsing between us, crying, stroking his head, looking at the face I would soon never set eyes on again. It is the finality of death that is the hardest.

By evening, Dad was trying to get out of bed to go home. The heart medication had taken effect, postponing his dying for the time being. I felt angry that the doctors couldn't just let him die, that they continued to fiddle with him in a war against death. I could not help but wonder if Dad wanted to go home to die in peace without any interference. However, the doctors convinced my mother that it was too late now to send him home, that she would be unable to handle the complications that would arise.

Days passed. Jon, Taylor, and I had to return to our own home, nearly a hundred miles away. Sobbing, I said good-bye to Dad, not knowing if I would see him again. I cried during the whole two-hour drive home. The tears of these weeks had a different quality than other tears; with my heart so open, the tears flowed spontaneously. They felt cleansing, even sweet.

CHAPTER 16

Release

Upon returning home, away from the distractions of the hospital, I felt much more in contact with Dad. In my journey that evening I was greeted by the tiger at the end of the tunnel.

> *He tells me to stroke him to regain my energy. As I stroke his fur and feel vitality restored, I notice a crystal hanging around his neck. Looking into it, I shift into swirling space. Then I am standing in a cavern of blue crystal with smooth, translucent walls. In one corner there is a large owl perched over a pool of golden pebbles.*
>
> *I ask the owl about Dad's death. Telepathically I hear the owl respond, "There is a time to die, a specific time that must be honored. When that time comes your father will die. Your father is now between the worlds. You will know when he passes, and then you must work with his spirit for seven days."*

Later I would learn that in many Native American traditions, the owl is the harbinger of death, while in Egyptian hieroglyphics the owl symbolizes night and death. It was fitting that the owl would speak about Dad's death. It had been difficult living with such uncertainty: When would Dad die? Would he be alone? Where would I be? However, the owl's words helped me to relax and trust that Dad would die in his own time.

I spent the next few days at home, meditating, being quiet, and focusing on Dad. I felt very much in tune with him. Then one morning I awakened knowing that I needed to visit him in the hospital. A friend of mine who had lost her father two years previously and understood what I was going through offered to drive me.

When we arrived at the hospital, it appeared that Dad would die that day. He had sunk deeply into the coma, his eyes staring through a gray film. His blood pressure was almost nonexistent, his skin white. He could hardly breathe through the fluid in his lungs. The smell of death pervaded the room. For days he had been disconnected from all life-support systems. He had had no water, no fluids, no medication. The nurses couldn't believe that he was still living.

I joined my mother at his bedside, feeling nauseated by the smell of the thick, yellow paste that he coughed up. I meditated, talking to him through my heart, synchronizing my breathing to his so that we breathed as one. Breathing in this way, I recalled a therapy session years before in which I had practiced Reichian breathing. Suddenly I had had no need or inclination to draw another breath; in that suspended state between breaths I had moved into a timeless state of great peace and heightened awareness. The boundaries of my body had dissolved into a sense of universal oneness. The Indian poet and mystic Kabir described this as "the place where the world is breathing."

A few hours later, as Dad's vital signs further waned, I read him Stephen Levine's dying meditation from *Who Dies?* His pauses in breathing synchronized with my talking as though he were listening intently.

> Take each breath as though it were the last. . . . Each breath the last breath. . . . Let go. Let yourself die. Don't hold on. . . . Let go into the light. Into the pure, open luminosity of your original nature. . . . Let go completely. Die gently into the light. . . . Free at last (pp. 244–45).

As I came to the words "Let go. Let yourself die," his breathing became agitated, as though he were fighting some inner battle. Dad was struggling toward death, contending with whatever threads still tied him to life.

I felt like a midwife, assisting my father in the supportive ways I could but unable to alleviate any of his inner turmoil. This was a battle he had to fight himself. I reflected back on my labor with my son; my midwife and my husband had supported me with their presence, but I alone had had to go through the hours of wracking pain. I had had to come up against and break through my own limitations; I had had to fight for the moment when I would hold my baby in my arms—just as Dad now struggled toward that moment of release.

Weeks before my son's birth, I had spent hours sitting at the bedside of a dying friend. Just as my friend was passing through the gate back to the Source, my child was coming through the other side. A few weeks after she died, I went into six hours of very intense labor. The intensity shocked me; I felt overwhelmed by the force moving through my body. Just like what I could see taking place in my father before me, a primal process had taken over then, and I was no longer in control of my body.

During Taylor's birth, Jon had sat with me, reminding me to breathe during contractions and to relax between them. I had felt I was struggling to stay afloat in a vast sea, riding over immense waves that threatened to submerge me if I started to panic. I had to flow with these tides without losing the rhythm, without losing awareness of each moment.

I had watched my mind searching desperately to escape this experience, yearning for a way out of this pain. The sounds of people going to a party had drifted up to the bedroom, carrying me for a minute to another world where there was laughter and no pain. Even that momentary distraction had thrown me out of rhythm, out of touch with my body, and I had entered the next contraction struggling, unprepared. As now I watched my father, so intently focused on making his passage, I felt I had found an experience from my own life that helped me understand his inner turmoil.

As Dad continued on his passage, the sounds of his labored gasps filling the room, vivid memories of my labor continued to flood through my mind. As I had reached the critical transition stage when the cervix is fully dilated, I had felt I'd reached my limit. I had been convinced I could go no further, and I had suddenly understood why women in hospitals were so prone to drugs and Cesareans at this stage. For a few minutes I had wanted anything that would make this pain stop. And then I recalled what it was that had brought me comfort and courage to go on, to press on further, beyond the pain.

With Jon's loving presence and gentle reminder that these feelings were very natural at this stage, I had reached deeper into myself and come upon new reserves of strength and courage. I had been pushed to my limit, or what I'd thought was my limit, only to find that the boundaries had moved out farther, beyond the concepts I'd had of myself.

As I sat with my father, I remembered how the realization had hit me years before that childbirth is an initiation out of which a mother is born, having suffered and died to her own limitations. And I began to see now that death itself is an initiation out of which we are born into pure spirit, breaking free of the limitations of the body.

The cervix in birth, just as the crown of the head in death, opens to allow heaven to pass through. Just as Dad now struggled in this critical transition, I had struggled in giving birth. After twenty minutes of pushing, feeling that my pelvis would split open, the baby, showing some signs of stress, had not moved. My midwife had asked me if I had any doubts that the baby could come out. Suddenly I'd realized that I had never moved past that point in my own birth: I had been pulled out with forceps.

I had had to work through this hurdle, even as I was exhausted from the hardest physical work I had ever undertaken. I had felt a shift taking place within me as I moved into new territory. As the midwife turned the little body, the baby had slipped through and been placed on my belly. He'd lifted his head and our eyes had met, seeing through each other into another space and time. For those first moments of life we had been together in a vast spaciousness and openness, a meeting like no other I've ever experienced.

And now Dad and I were together in a vast spaciousness. The

hospital room was filled with his presence as he lay comatose on the hospital bed. His body no longer could contain him. He flowed all around me and through me. Just as did those first days after Taylor's birth, the weeks during my father's dying propelled me into another realm, a sacred realm, in which all everyday concerns were swept clean by the naked power of pure love. Just as my newborn son had radiated a spacious purity, so Dad glowed with a holiness that left me in awe.

As the skies over the city began to darken in the late afternoon, Dad began to return to his body. His cheeks regained color, his hands grew warm, and his kidneys started functioning again; his blood pressure was up and his pulse strong and regular. This was a mystery to me, but perhaps Dad had drawn on my energy, for as he perked up I sank into exhaustion.

I had hoped that Mother and I could be with him when he died, but I remembered from my journey that I would not. That was one more picture of how I wanted him to die that I had to let go of. I prepared to leave, sobbing. I knew that this was the last time I would see him. I hugged and kissed him and left, only to run back to say good-bye again. Mother and I cried in each other's arms. She was feeling stronger from my visit and thanked me for being with her that day. When I arrived home, exhausted, I went on an inner journey to process the events of the day.

> *My guide tells me that my father had drawn on some of my energy to replenish his own waning life force. He directs me to jump into a lake of regeneration. As I do, the cold water tingles my body with energy. I dive to the bottom, finding a golden egg-shaped pebble. I swim with it to the surface, holding it up to the sunlight. My guide quietly informs me that something will emerge from this egg upon my father's passing.*

That night I had a dream in which a large redwood tree outside our house crashed to the ground during the night.

> I run outside to find our neighbor and his crew clearing the land. Where the redwood has been felled,

a vista has opened up so that I can see the valley
beyond. I am excited by the view, but then I see the
scarring of the earth from the excavation. I walk down
the hill to talk to the neighbor, but he is unwilling to
listen when I tell him he has no right to cut down a
tree on my land.

When I awakened from this dream, I immediately felt a
connection between the redwood and my father, both such
strong and imposing figures. The tree's crash to the ground felt as
earthshaking as Dad's death would be. His death would open up
new vistas and yet also leave me with open, raw wounds. My
relationship with the neighbor reminded me of how helpless I felt
as I confronted Dad's death—there is no negotiation. It is final
and irrevocable.

In the morning before school, Taylor wanted to make a
picture of his granddad. Taylor directed me to draw Granddad in
his hospital bed while he proceeded to draw Granddad's spirit to
one side of the page, looking on the hospital scene with a smile.
When Taylor left for school, I spent the day quietly meditating,
crying, and talking to Dad through my heart. I felt very close to
him in spirit, experiencing a luminous, clear space within my
heart. I thought often of the Sufi teacher Pir Vilayat Khan's
words, "You must needs leave that I may know you for your real
being."

In the afternoon I took a journey, the tiger leading me
through underground passageways to a silent cavern.

*A white-haired man sits down with me before a large
cistern in the middle of the cavern. In the still pool I see a
bright, shining light that explodes into twelve. The twelve
lights shine brightly for a while and then burst into a
multitude of lights. Then a luminous, bulging light begins
rising up from the depths of the cistern, from which a
naked baby emerges. I do not know what all this means,
and no explanation is forthcoming.*

*The tiger, man, and I leave for the hospital to visit
Dad. I am surprised to see Dad's power animal under his
bed. I realize that spent as she is, the little strength she has*

given Dad may have prevented Dad from dying. I love this animal and feel grateful for her loyalty and perseverance. Stroking her as I cry, I tell her that she must leave now.

The man directs me to stare into Dad's chest, and as I do, the light there grows stronger and brighter. Putting my hand on the crown of his head, I draw the light up and out of his body.

Then I reverently hold a radiant ball of light in my hands for a few seconds before it is swallowed by a great, limitless light. There is a dancing movement from within this, as though in celebration of a homecoming.

I am told that the form that Dad took in this life will never come again and that his spirit is now returned to the Infinite. The energy Dad has bequeathed to me as his child will soon be raining down upon me. The tiger takes me outside, pulling me down to the grass to be comforted by the earth.

That night I sat out under the stars, an endless, shimmering expanse of space. In the silence, I could feel my boundaries extending, stretching until I was one with the night sky, the spaciousness that is my essence and that unites all things. I had lit a candle in Dad's honor, and its light flickered against the window, as though it sought a place among the stars. In my heart I spoke to Dad as I cried cleansing tears. "Dad, your time has come to return home. You are even now dissolving into light and energy. Don't resist this; it is as natural as being born. I love you and I will miss you. But I feel connected to some essence of you that can never be taken away, a light that will always illuminate my heart." I felt a sharp pain in my chest, a jagged line cutting through the middle of my heart, wedging the two sides open. My heart was breaking open, and through that chasm the powerful light of love poured forth without limit.

Dad died the next afternoon with Mother at his side. I would have wanted to be meditating, perfectly in tune with his departure. So as fate would have it, I was at the dentist with Taylor, feeling very agitated that it was taking so long and upset that Taylor had sprouted seven cavities. I kept thinking to myself,

"How can this be taking so long when my father is dying?" I wanted to be home, meditating, waiting for Mother's call, but life demanded that I be in the middle of my duties.

When I returned home, there was a message from Mother that Dad had just died in her arms, her words barely distinguishable through the tears. Primal screams sprang from my gut. I wandered through the house crying out, pounding my chest, sobbing. Then I felt drawn to meditation and sank onto the floor. As soon as I closed my eyes, I felt a great peace and a sense of release. It seemed that Dad had gone on into the light without hesitation.

Throughout the afternoon I experienced waves of grief alternating with a sense of peace. In the evening, friends came to comfort me and to sing gospel songs. I called my mother, one of many calls that day as we shared our grief, and held up the receiver so she could hear us singing.

Later in the evening, my friends and I lay in the darkness to take a journey together, focusing on my father's passage.

> *My power animals are all there in the tunnel to greet me. They gather around me with such love and tenderness that I am moved to tears. At the end of the tunnel there is a brilliant light; my animals tell me that they will stay by me as I go into this light. They will call me back, for it is dangerous to stay there too long.*
>
> *I proceed into the light. Dad is there, luminous, with barely a form distinguishable. We hug with great love, wrapped in light. Then I see him sitting on a lotus burning in white fire, what is left of his form dissolving. The animals are calling me back, but I stay longer, ignoring their call.*
>
> *Jesus appears, light pouring from his heart, moving me beyond words. Dad has lost all form now and has merged into the light completely. The animals call again. I cannot break myself away. By the third call I leave, understanding now why they are here. The pull to stay is so strong.*
>
> *When I emerge from the light, my power animals surround me, each offering me a gift: the gifts of courage, of strength in my aloneness, of healing for myself and for*

*the earth, of transformation, of sight. A little bird alights
on the branch of a tree, so small and yet full of love and
sweetness. He flies to my shoulder and snuggles up against
my face. I sense Dad in his touch.*

*With the bird riding on my shoulder, I go down to
Xan's cave. He holds me as I cry and then looks deeply
into my eyes, saying, "You have prepared your father
well. From this day on, you will be changed. Your father,
as much as he loved you, was an inhibiting force in your
life. Just as he is free now, so you will experience a new
freedom. Let the grief flow over you like rain. Don't hold
on to it; let it come and go as it will. You will go through
many changes that have little to do with any of your
images of grieving."*

*Then he gently takes my hand and leads me to the
crystal cavern. I join the twelve and we all start to chant a
death chant, creating a strong vibration that lights the
crystals around the cavern.*

*Suddenly there is a shift and the cavern itself
illuminates, the stones trembling from some powerful
force like an earthquake. Through the center of the dome
an intense light pours down. We tilt back our heads, the
light touching our tongues. The light gathers in the center
and in a whirlwind passes back up through the dome. I
feel shaken yet blessed by the experience.*

*Xan moves to my side and gestures that it is time to
leave, leading me back to his cave. I lie down as he places
an herb on my tongue. When I have rested, he tells me to
go outside and be by myself.*

*I step outside the cave, sitting alone under a vast
blanket of stars. The flaming infinity above me provides a
knowing backdrop to the feelings in my heart, exposing a
terrifying aloneness and yet providing a strange comfort. I
feel embraced by boundless space, kissed by twinkling
stars. I call out, "Dad, I love you! Good-bye!"*

CHAPTER 17

Talking Through Your Heart

At some point your parent will begin to pass through the stages of dying, step by step loosening the ties to the body. For longer and longer periods he or she may seem to slip into another world, the eyes turning inward. The periods of connection with ordinary reality grow shorter, the chances to interact and talk less and less frequent. Finally your parent may shift into a coma state. Since you are no longer able to reach your parent in the old ways of relating, this can be a lonely and frustrating time.

The resources you have developed in your sanctuary time become invaluable. Having learned to sit with yourself just as you are, embracing whatever feelings and thoughts surface, you may feel more prepared to sit with your parent dying, watching the natural flow of events without interfering. Having sorted out your own expectations from the reality of the situation, you may have moved into more acceptance that your parent needs to die in his or her own way, not according to your pictures of how you would like it to happen. Whatever unfinished business you have dealt with will lessen your investment in your parent's staying alive for you. You will feel more ready to let your parent move on. If you have been exploring entering other worlds yourself, you may be more able to support your parent in the passage out of this world; you may be more appreciative of the mystery and less frightened of the unknown.

As we sit down next to our parent in the last hours and days or tune into him or her from afar, we enter into a sacred space of transition, a threshold. We come prepared and unprepared. In the face of a great mystery and of a great loss, we tremble, wondering how we will make it through. The old structures can no longer serve us, for they cannot embrace the immensity that looms before us. Our challenge is to enter the unknown, moment by moment, and trust that an inner knowing will guide us step by step through our parent's dying.

To contact that inner knowing you will need to take time to tune in, listening in the silence to the "still small voice within" with a willingness to expand beyond known boundaries.

Sit down, close your eyes, and settle into your body. Let go of all distractions, worries, and concerns, and bring your full attention to your body. Notice any sensations—heat, cold, tinglings, vibrations. Notice areas of tension or relaxation, hardening or softening. Become aware of your breathing, how full or constricted it is, how deep or shallow.

If you have been holding yourself together, give yourself permission now to let go and to feel fully what is going on physically and emotionally—let yourself feel all the tensions, contractions, frustrations, anger, and sadness just as they are. Let go into the pain. Make room for whatever is happening in this moment. Make room in your heart for your grief.

Now move your attention to the sound of your parent's breathing. If you are not with your parent, you can imagine this; the breathing may be labored, raspy, or relaxed. Synchronize your breathing with your parent's, breathing in and out together. As you do this, feel his or her struggle, as though something within were laboring to free itself, as the last ties to this world are painfully severed.

Somewhere in this struggle you may sense that your parent is hesitant to die because of you, or you may recognize your own unwillingness to let go. If this is so, explore your resistance or reassure your parent that he or she can move on now.

Begin now to let go of the physical form with which you have identified your parent. Breathing in and out in rhythm with your parent's breathing, sense that form dissolving into spaciousness, the room filling with a vibrant energy.

Your parent is now flowing all around you and through you, free, expansive, alive, full of love. Stay with this, treasuring how connected you have been and always will be.

Physical distance or the state of coma do not have to block access to your dying parent if you are willing to explore the other possibilities for connection and communion that go beyond our habitual means. Meditation, shamanic journey, and active imagination all are potent resources, but just being in a receptive state may be enough to tune you in to your parent. It is not unlike tuning your radio dial to a certain frequency. You may have to play with the dial for a while, patiently sorting through other stations and static until you finally come to the one you had been looking for.

When a parent is separated by distance, in a coma, or unwilling to communicate, you can talk to him or her silently through your heart. Stephen Levine has used this method with many people who were dying with powerful results.

Recently a client called to thank me for our work together during the illness of her father. In our sessions, we had discussed her feelings about his death, her unfinished business with him, and her frustrations that she was unable to communicate with him about his illness. Her father, though failing rapidly, was not told by the doctors that his cancer had spread and that he was dying. I suggested that she could say what she needed to say to him by talking to him through her heart—even though he was 3,000 miles away. In her first efforts she felt awkward doing this, but she persisted because it felt healing to her.

Then, on the night before she was to visit him, she had a vivid dream in which her father appeared, telling her, "I know what the doctors won't tell me. I'm all right, so don't worry about me. Remember to put oil in your car and get your tires changed every 30, 000 miles." She awakened knowing that she had made contact with him, that he had heard what she had been communicating to him through her heart. At peace now with his dying, she was able to sit with him with an open heart while her brother was unable even to come into the room. He died a few days later.

There are often confirmations, like this dream, that communication channels are open. Many of these are so subtle that they escape detection because we are not alert. For example, as you communicate to a parent who is in a coma, you may see subtle signs of response in a flicker of an eyelid, a pause in breathing, a slight movement of the hand. Arnold Mindell, author of *Coma,* proposes that we can learn through careful attention to these signals to communicate with people in comas. He demonstrates through vivid case histories that coma is not an inaccessible state but instead an altered state of consciousness with great potential for healing, whether into death or into life.

There is so much more going on while your parent is dying than meets the eye. If you are willing to explore and experiment, you can become a part of this major transition, supporting and guiding your parent through the birth canal. Your parent has outgrown the body, just as an infant outgrows the womb. It is a natural process to leave the body—as natural as it is to come into it at birth—wrenching and painful as it may be. It may help to remind your parent of this, supporting him or her in letting go and moving into the unknown, into the light. It may be helpful to read aloud a passage from some tradition or teaching that clarifies this, such as Stephen Levine's guided meditation on dying in *Who Dies?*

Then the moment comes: The last breath. Release. We feel relieved from our vigil yet filled with loss. We feel separated from our parent—no more opportunities for that last talk, for that encounter we had longed for. And the grief wells up in us, not just from this loss but from all the losses, all the incompletions, the unexpressed love, the death of pets and friends, the disappointments, the failure of hopes and dreams, the unshed tears, the unlived moments. It is our challenge to embrace all this grief, not to shrink from it, to trust the feelings as they present themselves, not to judge them and put them away. Certain feelings that are very common in grief, such as guilt, anger, and relief, may be more difficult to accept.

In the hours and days following the death you may feel swept into a chaotic sea of uncontrollable emotions, thoughts, and physical reactions. You may be subject to sleeplessness, fatigue, loss of appetite, depression, moodiness, intense emotions welling suddenly and as suddenly subsiding, thoughts spinning. Your mind may seem consumed with the events around the death, going over and over the words said or not said, the actions taken or not taken, the last encounter, the last words exchanged. Disturbing images may haunt you. Or if you were not with your parent at the moment of death, you may feel guilty that you were not there or cheated of those last moments together. Sometimes, even when there has been a constant vigil by family members, a parent may slip quietly away when everyone has left the room for a brief break. These thoughts can mobilize feelings of shame, regret, guilt, and anger.

As all this is happening, you may feel out of control, seized by some great force that relentlessly pushes you farther and farther along a dark passage. Then you may realize that you too are dying to old restrictions and outgrown ways of being. You too are struggling through the birth canal. An old world has been left behind; there is no going back.

CHAPTER 18

Broken Glass, Splintered Wood

As Xan had told me, the days and weeks following my father's death brought many changes that I did not expect. I often felt shaken by the realization that I would never see Dad's face again. While the images from the journeys remained vivid, I never felt his presence. I did not even dream about him. I had the strong sense that he had passed on to other realms without looking back—as though he had business to attend to in another world.

As I felt Dad was free, I too felt a new freedom that was a surprise to me. My heart wide open, intense feelings and energy surged through me at unexpected moments. A flood of tears, a burst of joy, an explosion of anger. Just as suddenly as they had come, they would pass, leaving me bewildered. At times I was overcome with a deep sadness, at others with a profound peace.

In grief one is carried by this flood of feelings and experiences. My mind, bobbing up and down in this vast river, struggled for control and understanding, desperately trying to hold on to a concept that was at least familiar. Propelled downstream, unable to catch hold of anything solid, I was learning to surrender to the rushing currents of the river, tumultuous, unpredictable, and chaotic as they were. There were days when the currents pulled me underwater into a dark murkiness; other days I floated peacefully, warmed by the sun.

Dad's death challenged me to enter fully into the stream of life by shattering the world as I had known it and tearing down the boundaries I had carefully erected to feel more secure and in control. For weeks I longed for that illusion of security; I was amazed at how subtly my parents had buffered me from the deep realization of my own mortality, of the fragility of life, of my aloneness in this vast universe.

My dreams supported me in my passage out of the old structures, acknowledging the need to tear down the old to make way for the new vision. Shortly after my father's death, I had a dream in which a man was helping me to remodel my house, an appropriate image for the inner process at work during grief.

> The man insists upon removing the boards that cover a line of windows in the living room; I resist his suggestion, unable to visualize what the outcome will be. Since he is so insistent and seems confident in his vision of the remodeling, I finally give in.
> He pries the wood loose and commences to shatter the glass. I am horrified at the sound, skeptical of what could possibly emerge out of this chaos of broken glass and splintered wood. And yet when he is finished, I am pleased with the result, glad that he had the vision to make this change. The room is now full of light, graced with three lovely windows.

This dream suggested that old structures needed to be torn apart and renovated, creating a temporary chaotic state. Something in me would have to be wrenched loose and shattered, but this would eventually result in a new spaciousness and lightness of being. I was reminded of the words of my professor in college, Norman O. Brown: "There is no breakthrough without breakage." A part of my psyche already envisioned that change and insisted upon it; another part resisted, unable to see past the old structures. But finally my resistance passed and I just let it happen.

A few weeks after my father's death, the almond tree in our garden burst into bloom, lovely, translucent white blossoms gracing the once barren limbs. They did not hold back when there was life to be expressed; they gave themselves totally to those few weeks of blossoming, without any anticipation that soon their petals would be scattered on the earth. They were willing to enter this stream of life wholeheartedly.

I grieved that, unlike these blossoms, I held back on life, that I did not give myself fully to each moment. As the weeks progressed, my grief began to focus not as much on my father as on my own unlived life. I began to weep for myself, for all the losses, all the hurts, all the unexpressed love.

This grieving over my own life unlived initiated a descent to the underworld, to the deep inner recesses of my psyche. However, I found I could not hide or lose myself in this darkness. A powerful light shone mercilessly into those recesses, revealing lifelong family patterns that had conditioned me to limit myself and hold back on life, patterns I had never before seen so clearly, in spite of years of therapy. I was seeing with new eyes and could not believe I had been so blind. In a poetry reading I attended during this time, I heard Robert Bly share his own inner struggles and insights into his family during his father's illness and death. He made a powerful statement that resonated with my own experience: "There are times in life when we see our family patterns for what they are and that is a dark moment."

For months there were many dark moments as I struggled to integrate the painful insights that were breaking into my awareness. Meanwhile, my mother was turning to me in her grief, suffering with many unresolved issues from her marriage. We had emotionally supported each other through the tumultuous time of my father's dying, sharing a closeness that I had been grateful for. But now I realized the danger of being swept into her experience of grief when I needed to honor my own. I began to see more clearly than I ever had the dysfunctional role I played in our relationship, sacrificing my own needs and feelings to take care of hers. The feelings that surged through me in my grief could not, would not, be set aside; they cried out to be fully experienced. At the very time Mother was seeking my support, I was needing to stand apart and feel my aloneness. I had never felt so alone.

As I pulled away, albeit gently, we began to fight. This was also not according to my concepts of grief. At the time my mother needed me so much, I was unable to be there for her in the old way. It did not make sense to change lifelong patterns with her at such a critical time. But the grief was not reasonable; the river swept me into new, uncharted territory. Perhaps this is the window of opportunity that comes with a parent's death—for those brief months when one is so wide open in grief, one can delve into territories that were previously inaccessible.

As the drama of the gods lives on in our psyches, I recognized how I had been living out the archetypal mother-daughter drama portrayed so vividly in the Demeter-Persephone myth. Demeter and Persephone were inseparable as mother and daughter until Hades, the god of the underworld, stole Persephone away. Demeter, goddess of corn and of the harvest, turned the verdant earth into a frozen wasteland in her anger and bitterness.

The gods sought to remedy this dire situation, for nothing would grow and the people were starving; finally, the lord of the underworld made a compromise. For four months of every year, Persephone would reign over her own domain in the underworld. With the coming of spring, earth celebrated with new life the reunion of mother and daughter, although now a daughter who was a woman in her own right.

The descent into the underworld of grief had changed my world, as it had Persephone's. I had wandered for months in a dark land, alone, overwhelmed by the vision of the underside of things. What I had seen and learned in that dark time had prepared me for a new relationship to my mother and to my own womanhood.

This healing was reflected in a journey in which my mother appeared, holding out to me a rose of indescribable beauty. Layers of rich red petals curled back like crested waves, revealing a tender pink cluster nestled at the center. Lifting my eyes to my mother's face, I could feel the movement of that rose resonating in the depths of my being; its opening was my opening. Then she shared with me many things involving the future that I will not disclose here.

Later in the journey the meaning of this rose was revealed:

*I am standing in a rose garden, surrounded by hundreds
of beautiful roses of all colors and in all stages of growth.
Some are small, tight green globes, while others shyly
reveal but a sliver of color. In some, silken petals form
brilliant chalices that rise up out of beds of sturdy green
sepals. Others bask in full blossom, great, soft petals
unfurled in a blaze of breathtaking color.*

*A small man dressed in earthen tones bends over one
bush to my right, pruning with rhythmic strokes. He turns
to me as he becomes aware of my presence. "Welcome!"
Waving his hand in a sweeping motion, he directs my gaze
to the roses. I notice now that the garden extends down
the hill, thousands of roses spreading out to the horizon in
blazing swatches of color. The man says, "Each of these
roses is a relationship in some stage of growth. With
nurturing and care, many will blossom." As this
innovative concept begins to penetrate, I look again at the
roses with new eyes, feeling profoundly moved. The man
gestures with a muddy, callused hand to a flame-colored
rose in full bloom. "Every relationship and every rose
blooms to the glory of God. The rose your mother gave
you was from this garden."*

*I cannot speak, stunned by the impact of his words.
The rose of our relationship had been cultivated, nurtured,
and pruned in this garden. My mother had come to show
me how it was now beginning to blossom. As my eyes
wander from bush to bush, I am overcome by the power
of each rose, the meeting place of two hearts.*

Because I felt overwhelmed by the magnitude of all these
changes, I often needed to withdraw into the sanctuary I had
created in our bedroom. On a shelf over my bed I had placed
Dad's picture with a lucky coin he had treasured, along with a
statue of St. Francis, candles, and flowers. Sitting there, I could
open fully to the experience of my grief, tend to my wounds, and
integrate the rapid shifts in my world.

As my son, husband, and friends went about their lives,
engaged in their daily pursuits, I sometimes felt that I was in a
dream, that I would wake up, my father would be alive, and my
life would go on. However, sitting before the picture of my

father, I was faced with the reality of my father's death and of the irreversible changes in my world. Whether I cried, talked to Dad, wrote, took a shamanic journey, meditated, or just sat with myself, I felt a healing taking place deep inside.

As I rose to leave, I was better prepared to enter the world, to reach out to friends and family, play a game with my son, see a client, or cook dinner. Unexpectedly, as I engaged in these activities, a feeling of sorrow might flood my heart and tears fill my eyes, but I was learning to accept the tides of grief that came and went with their own timing.

CHAPTER 19

Tending to Your Wounds

The time right after a parent's death is a vulnerable, raw, and chaotic time. It is a time of major transition for both of you as old worlds are left behind. Many cultures have acknowledged this time with rituals for guiding the deceased on and for insulating those who are grieving. Since many of these rituals are no longer available to us, it is important to prepare your own.

Defining and creating a sacred space is a critical initial step in any ritual; so it is for grieving. As was discussed in a previous chapter, there is a tremendous potential for healing and change if the powerful forces unleashed in grief are contained and directed into channels of transformation.

If you have not established a sanctuary space yet, go back and reread Chapter Four. If you have already established your sanctuary but have used it only sporadically, then this is a time to use it again on a daily basis.

As the weeks pass, there will be shifts in your grieving that affect how you choose to spend your sanctuary time. The first days, or even weeks, of sanctuary time may be a time of great emotional upheaval and release—even if it has been years since your parent died. Many clients found that just sitting down before their parent's picture, having given themselves the permission to grieve, triggered a flood of tears or rage. Gradually these emotional eruptions may become interspersed with periods of exploring and integrating the changes that are occurring in your life. Then it might feel appropriate to focus on unfinished business with the deceased parent, changes in the family system, and new perspectives.

As you finally begin to emerge from the dark middle phase of grief, you may feel a strong urge for expression during your sanctuary time, perhaps an urge to dance, sing, or write. Or you may feel drawn to explore different methods for expanding your world, such as shamanic journey, active imagination, and meditation. However, at this time you may feel less and less need of the sanctuary time, as you move back into the mainstream of life. You may feel the need for more social contact and involvement in various activities.

No matter what stage of grief you are passing through, events in your inner or outer life may call out for your attention during sanctuary time. Perhaps your body is tight and your breathing constricted. Then you may need to breathe deeply and relax your body. Or you may discover that your thoughts gravitate toward a disturbing event, perhaps something a family member or friend said or did. Or a memory of your parent may have just brought more feelings to the surface. Or you may have had a dream the night before that you want to explore.

As the sanctuary time comes to a close each day, reflect on what has occurred, savoring any new insights, noticing again the feelings that are stirring within. Clarify for yourself how you can best take care of yourself that day as you step out into the world from your sanctuary.

Following the sanctuary time, you may want more time alone, whether just to sit or to take a walk. You may feel raw and vulnerable and need to curtail outside commitments. As you go about the activities of the day, the grief may surface from time to time in waves, prompting a need for a brief retreat—you may want to close your eyes for a few minutes, step into another room, or shift the conversation to share what is going on with you.

You may want the company of friends or family. It is important to reach out during grief—to share, to ask for help and support, to give and receive love. Relationships can deepen to new levels of richness and love as old boundaries and walls fall away. There just isn't the energy available to sustain the old patterns of holding and distancing—nor is there a desire to. Many clients have shared a dramatic change in their former values: they have seen that in the end, as everything falls away, the priority of love becomes clear and undisguised.

However, there may be disappointments and surprises in your relationships. While your friends often have the best intentions in trying to help you, some may be unwilling or unable to support you in your work with your grief. They may prefer giving their advice to just being with you in whatever state you are in. They may tell you, "You've been wallowing in your grief. Get out and do something. Forget about it." Some of your friends may simply withdraw. It takes courage to be with someone in grief, and many are not up to it—the vulnerability and lack of control can be frightening, the intensity of feelings overwhelming. Other friends or even acquaintances may step forward to be with you with sensitivity and caring that you never expected from them.

You will need to take care of your needs in these situations. Communicate your hurt, and clarify for your friends what you want from them; for example, you might say, "I need for you just to listen to me right now and not give me advice. . . . I want you to hold me. . . . Would you be willing to be with my kids for a while so that I can have a break? . . . I want to be alone now."

As you turn to your family for comfort or support, your expectations may again collide with reality. If you are seeking some stability and continuity in your family, you probably will be disappointed to find that it too is undergoing major changes and shifts.

The family acts to maintain a balance in its relationships. Any change, even a seemingly insignificant one, upsets that balance, resulting in a temporary state of chaos that is very threatening to the family members. Many family therapists have observed that the family functions as a basically conservative system, resisting change even when it is for the good of the family.

With the death of one of the parents, the family that has evolved over years into an established and predictable system is thrown into chaos and upheaval. The old patterns no longer work with the same predictable results. Often, unhealthy patterns come to light that had been hidden in and obscured by the old structure. These new insights can be very shocking, surprising, and disturbing. For months the family members may thrash around, seeking a new balance with one another; this can be a very tumultuous experience in the midst of grief.

There is a brief window of opportunity right after a parent's death, when the family is opened up to change before a new system is established. You can either be thrown into the new system or consciously participate in creating new patterns that are healthy for you. You can begin to speak up for what you want, explore new ways of relating, and cut through old patterns that are trying to reestablish themselves. Many have found it helpful to seek out a family therapist at this time, to support the movement of the family into a new, healthier system.

These changes in your family and the loss of your parent signal that it is time for you to learn to parent yourself, to give yourself the direction, encouragement, nurturance, protection, and affection that you may have sought outside yourself. Even though we may not look to our parents for active parenting once we become adults, we may have fallen into the habit of expecting that someone else will make things better, protect us, and give us what we will not give ourselves.

You may want to take this time to define and evaluate what your parents gave you that you are now unwilling to give yourself, what you wanted from your parents that they were unable to give you, and what your parents gave you that you never acknowledged. This helps to separate your expectations from the reality of your relationship and to define qualities of parenting that you now want to nurture and develop in yourself.

We all have expectations of our parents that they could never fulfill, just as they had certain expectations of us as their children. Once these expectations are clarified and we acknowledge our disappointment, we can begin to see the relationship for what it was. We can begin to appreciate what our parents did give us and accept what they didn't. Are there qualities you always judged or disliked in your parent, qualities that from a new perspective can become strengths in your life? Are there qualities you admired in your parent that you now want to develop in your own life? Look for opportunities in your daily life to begin developing these qualities. For example, perhaps your mother was nurturing and supportive whenever you felt depressed or sick. Can you learn now to give yourself that nurturance that you may so need at this time?

Are there ways that your parent related to you that you have already internalized unconsciously? Evaluate these—do they work for you now? Perhaps you had never recognized that what you admired or disliked in your parent is already integrated into your own personality structure. Perhaps your parent was extremely critical—whatever you did was not good enough. You may find that you now treat yourself as critically as your parent did. This is a good time to challenge these destructive patterns; learn to give yourself compassion and understanding, perhaps saying to yourself, "You don't have to do this perfectly. Relax. Enjoy yourself. Don't worry about the mistakes."

As you confront the reality of the relationship with your parent, you also need to work with the expectations. These may have been a continuing source of disappointment, frustration, anger, and bitterness. At this point it is important to acknowledge that these expectations come from within you. Somewhere deep inside, you hold an image of what you want your parent to be. Instead of trying to mold your parent into that image, work with contacting that image and letting it work on you.

These images are often archetypal in origin, stemming from a collective source in the psyche. Throughout the history of humanity there have been references to the Great Mother and Father or, as Jungian analyst Erich Neumann calls them, the "World Parents." Carl Jung studied these archetypes extensively. He was fascinated that they appeared over and over in ancient myths and religions as well as in the dreams of his patients.

Through active imagination techniques and shamanic journeys, many of my clients have been able to contact these archetypal parents, who could provide love, support, and guidance. Sometimes these bore resemblance to their parents in ordinary reality, but more often they were very different. It is important to understand that these archetypal parents are not substitutes for parents in our daily life; they are living presences within us.

For example, my teacher in shamanic journeys, Xan, was an archetypal father for me, although it took a while for me to recognize this. He was a consistent support throughout my father's illness, knowing just what I needed in each stage of grief. He didn't seek to protect me from my pain but had the wisdom and vision to help me move through it. It was not my survival or comfort that he sought but my transformation. It wasn't until just before my father's death that it suddenly occurred to me that as I was losing a father in one world I was gaining one in another. My relationship with Xan continues to unfold in my journeys, my love and respect for him deepening as I am exposed to his wisdom, compassion, and guidance.

One client suffered deeply after her mother's death, because she had never received the loving and nurturing she had wanted from her mother. She had grown up craving attention, comfort, and touching. However, her mother was a reserved, stiff woman who, though she had other gifts to give, could not give her the warmth she needed. As an adult, my client's neediness frightened away her friends and lovers, as she sought desperately to fill the empty place she felt deep within.

In our sessions, she began to grieve that her needs had not been satisfied and then to accept that she would never receive from her mother the kind of loving she had so wanted as a child. This acceptance released her into the present, where as an adult she could begin to explore new possibilities for love and nurturance.

New images began to take form in active imagination exercises, vivid images of a mother who held and stroked her and listened attentively to her. She was profoundly moved by this experience; her body softened and throbbed with joy. In one session I guided her through a birth experience. Moving down the birth canal to the natural rhythm of contractions, she emerged into the world, exhausted though wide open with wonder. Her archetypal mother, looking very different than the one in ordinary reality, reached out for her, holding, caressing, and soothing her. For a long time she lay in her mother's arms, drinking in the love. When she opened her eyes, her face was flushed, soft, and glowing with an inner sense of well-being. From that new base she looked out on a world different than the one she had known—responsive, alive, and loving.

In subsequent sessions, she contacted this mother again and again in her imagination, participating in the evolution of a relationship that was full of support, love, and touching. The old feelings of bitterness and resentment toward her mother that had haunted her grief began to dissolve, and they were replaced by a surprising new sense of tenderness and forgiveness.

The following exercise will give you the opportunity to meet your archetypal parent.

Take a few full breaths and then close your eyes. Bring your attention to your body, noticing the sensations that are taking place in this moment. Notice areas of warmth or cold, of tension or relaxation, of tingling or numbness.

Now become aware of the sensations you are experiencing as you float in a womb—a dark, wet, soft space. Enjoy playing, tumbling, and stretching in this small sea.

Now you are growing larger, and the womb is feeling more confined; you curl up to fit into the shrinking space. You are beginning to feel uncomfortable.

Then the contractions begin, mild at first, as the walls of the uterus press in on your body. Then they grow stronger and more insistent. You feel pushed, pressed, and squeezed by some great force into a narrow passage. You are leaving the world you had known. Where are you going? Are you dying?

Suddenly, you are released—your head is free, and you are looking into the faces of loving beings. One final pressure and your body slips into comforting hands. Your mother holds you tenderly, stroking your skin as she looks into your eyes. You can see great love there, and you can feel it in her touch. Take some time just to be with her as she welcomes you into the world. Receive her love, absorbing it in every cell of your body.

Then your father bends down and his strong yet gentle hands lift you to his chest. He cradles you there, holding you close, looking into your eyes. Take your time as you fully experience this time with your father as he meets you for the first time.

Maintaining a connection with this sense of well-being, knowing that deep within, you are loved, protected, and cherished, look out on the world with new eyes. This archetypal parent is living within you now, ready to be contacted again and again.

———————————

CHAPTER 20

The Phone Call

There seemed to be triggers to my grief—particularly holidays and birthdays. Opening the mailbox on my birthday, I felt excited as I reached for the bundle of mail, thinking it held the cards my father always sent me, a ritual we had enjoyed since I was a child. The cards had arrived, sometimes one by one, sometimes all at once, each one signed in his graceful, open handwriting, "Love, Daddy." But then my heart sank as I remembered that there would be no card from my father on this birthday, or on any others. I walked back to the house, sobbing.

On Father's Day, Jon's words to his father, "Hi, Dad. Happy Father's Day," jabbed at the wound in my heart, releasing a flood of tears. One year earlier I had said those same words to my father. Now I no longer had a father to call. I was struck that for Jon this was such an ordinary moment, that his family was safe and intact while mine was now fragmented.

That afternoon Jon, Taylor, and I had brunch on a terrace overlooking a small pond full of colorful carp. As Jon and I ate, Taylor played at the water's edge. Suddenly he called out, "Look! That fish reminds me of Granddad—the dead one!" He pointed excitedly to an orange and black striped carp that was swimming under his outstretched hand.

I felt a comfort in Taylor's reminder that Dad is a part of the earth. As I stood by the pond I looked to see for myself what reminded Taylor of his granddad in that carp. But even more than seeing characteristics that might be similar—a sense of

113

leadership, strength, purpose—I realized in that moment that Dad was now a part of the earth, and if I looked carefully I could see him all around me.

I remembered that a few months before, I had held Dad's ashes in my hands, feeling humbled and shocked that his once strong and virile body was now reduced to a few handfuls of gray, powdery ash and little chunks of bone. Palm outstretched, I watched reverently as the warm wind swept the ashes from my hand, scattering them over the surface of the sea in a trail of silvery dust. Then the water gently lapped over and the ashes were gone. Just as his spirit had been received into the infinite light on the day of his death, now his body was received back into the earth. His body had come home to his mother, the earth. There I would find him in rock and river, in fish and feather.

Mother Earth can take on a new role in one's life after a parent's death—the parent continues on through her in a vast cycle of life and death. When a parent falls away, one's foundation crumbles, but then one can discover that one has always been supported and sustained by another ground, the earth.

The earth became a living presence in my life. I rejoiced in her beauty; she gave me comfort, sustenance, and strength. She lured me into her heart, introducing me to the helpers in the invisible world who were devoted to helping her through this time of transition.

A carp, similar to the one Taylor had pointed out, became my guide in a shamanic journey, leading me down into the earth.

I finally come to rest on a moist mound of earth in complete darkness. I wait, shifting uneasily. There is a stirring from under me, and a large eyeball emerges. As I look through it, I am able to see what others cannot in times of darkness. It is now apparent that golden strands lead up from this pit, creating a net from which I cannot fall. The sun begins to shine within the darkness, growing steadily more intense. And my body begins to shake.

I pass out, and I experience darkness followed by a sensation of floating through white. I'm in a stone cave facing a breathtaking stone carving of the sun. I am told that the sun is a channel of galactic information; when the sun shines in the heart, that galactic information is passed to the cells. I look up; in the middle of the carving of the sun is a hole. Against my better judgment, I feel impelled to put my finger in that hole. As I do, there is a sharp pain in my finger. I draw it out—there are two bloody slices through my finger. Something has bit me!

All at once I pass through a rain of light that dissolves my body into dancing, shimmering cells, millions of brilliant humming dots, each with its own consciousness and yet all functioning together as one. They speak to me: "You must listen to us, pay close attention to us, for we are struggling to awaken. You must learn to communicate with us. We may be small, but each one of us contains the entire universe. Feel us within you humming, dancing in the great flow of life. Find the dark places where some of us rest in fear and trauma, arouse us into life, shower us with your love and attention. Not one of us can be left in darkness in this dance of awakening. We ask this of you not only for yourself, but also for the earth. She too is stirring with new life as we awaken in her."

Then I am standing once again before the stone carving. A green snake emerges from the hole, wrapping itself around the sun.

That green snake was to appear again in future journeys, each time eliciting from me the same fascination and horror. I sensed that it was set on some unknown mission, perhaps to instill in me some change of attitude or new awareness. To this end it seemed willing to wound or shock me.

Snakes have been a potent symbol of healing and transformation in many cultures. As Carl Jung states in his *Collected Works,* "the idea of transformation and renewal by means of a serpent is a well-substantiated archetype" (vol. XIII, par. 184). In ancient Greece, snakes were associated with healing, vitalizing the temple of Asklepius, the god of healing, with their presence. Today the logo of the medical profession depicts a snake wrapped around the staff of Asklepius. The transformational aspect is evident in yogic practices of India that sought to activate the sleeping serpent, kundalini. Then it would rise along the spine, opening and transforming all the energy centers or chakras in its path. When the kundalini finally rose to the top of the head, the person could achieve illumination.

This journey addressed not only my own healing and transformation but also that of the earth. Several story lines were developing over time in my journeys. One was more personal, involving the drama of my father's death and the subsequent changes in my life. In the other, the earth's transformation was revealed piece by piece. With each journey I added a piece to the magnificent puzzle that lay spread before me; gradually, small sections were coming to life, hinting at a larger mystery. I had already seen images of new life being forged in the center of the earth, of light pushing its way out. I had seen the earth struggling to give birth, agonizing in labor.

There was always the danger of attempting to see these images through the eyes of ordinary reality, to interpret them literally. This hidden reality cannot be confused with the one we experience in ordinary reality; it is, as Jungian analyst Patricia Berry emphasized, "real in its own way but never because it corresponds to something outer." These images, so powerful and pure in their presentation, shriveled under the critical eye of judgment; they resisted any attempts to squeeze them into the context of ordinary reality, any temptation to use them for predictive purposes. From a mythic perspective, however, they could suggest new possibilities of the evolving myth of our planet. In his book *The Final Choice*, Michael Grosso suggests that "visions are given to assist humanity at large in the transition to new forms of life. The earth itself is in need of transformation; we need to learn to adapt to a new earth because the old earth is passing away" (pp. 314–15).

The months passed; gradually I was entering back into life, into a richer and vaster life than I had known before, animated with many realities and many worlds. I found wonder and mystery in the rocks in my garden, the flight of a bird, the sun-kissed golden leaves falling to the ground, my son's animated face. Stepping into our garden or into my husband's arms, I felt I was entering an intimate rhythm at the heart of things, love welling up in a great surge of joy that it was all so simple and natural and yet so mysterious.

The great river of grief swept on underground. Standing on the earth, I could feel it rumbling deep under my feet, occasionally spewing up through crevices with geyser force. Then I might dissolve into tears or become very quiet and introspective—or dream about Dad. One night, eight months after my father's death, I had a significant dream about him.

> Mother and I are in a restaurant. The owner approaches our table, saying, "The mister is on the phone." I am surprised, as I know that Dad is dead. Mother jumps up and goes to the phone.
>
> When she has finished, I go. I pick up the receiver, wondering if it will really be Dad on the other end. As I hear his voice so clearly, with all its intonations, my doubts are swept away. "Hi, Dad," I say. He seems disoriented, asking, "Taylor?" I respond, "No, it's me." As he pauses, I feel afraid that he has forgotten me. I ask him, "How are you?" He pauses again and says, "It's been hard lately over here." I can hear pain in his voice. I want to reach out to him, hold his hand, give him comfort, but I feel frustrated and helpless before the boundary dividing the land of the living from the land of the dead. I feel so close to him and yet so far away. I begin to cry. I say, "I miss you, Dad." Then I replace the receiver.

I awoke immediately, certain that I had made contact with my father for the first time since his death. His voice, so clear, reached through the dream and touched my heart in that place that knows no boundaries. I realized that it was close to Halloween, the time when the boundary between the worlds is thin.

That morning I took a journey. I was concerned about Dad and the pain he was in. This was perplexing to me, as it seemed he had moved on so quickly after his death, in great peace. I won-

dered whether there might be stages to the after-death experience, different levels of passage.

> *The coyote meets me at the tunnel entrance, leading me up*
> *a few levels to a place of light where Dad is waiting alone.*
> *We are both very happy to see one another; simultaneous*
> *smiles break out on our faces. As he embraces me, I can*
> *sense that he is softer, more vulnerable than he was in life.*
>   *Something has changed in my relationship to him; I*
> *have a new acceptance of his humanness, of his frailties*
> *and deceptions. My heart has room for it all, and I feel*
> *freed of wanting him to be any different than he was.*
> *When I tell him about my dream, he confides in me that it*
> *has been hard for him lately seeing the hurt he caused in*
> *his life and being unable to do anything about it. I remind*
> *him that he can forgive himself as well as send love to*
> *those he hurt in his life. As I put my hand on his chest, I*
> *can feel energy and light pouring into his heart. He takes*
> *my hand and then we say good-bye.*

Death, though changing the temple of my father's life, had
not terminated our relationship, which continued to unfold and
change.

A month later, around Thanksgiving, I sank into a dark
depression. Upon reflection, I came to the realization that the
depression had started precisely a year after I learned of Dad's
cancer. It was as though my very cells carried this memory,
stirred into a dance of mourning upon the anniversary of this
crisis. Clear images of the agonizing stages of Dad's illness sur-
faced regularly; my body throbbed with all the anxiety, fears,
helplessness, and horror I had felt. I had noticed for years that
clients very often sank into depression on the anniversary of a
parent's death, even years later when they had consciously for-
gotten the date. The body remembers.

The depression continued for weeks, as I wandered aimlessly
and listlessly in the underworld. Every morning I awakened to
the same dark sky. Often I cried out in protest, "Why am I still
feeling this way?" At the same time I knew that I simply needed
to surrender to and trust the invisible workings of the psyche.

Again and again I turned to a passage in *Four Quartets* by T. S. Eliot for comfort and support through this dark time:

> I said to my soul, be still, and let the dark come upon you
> Which shall be the darkness of God. As, in a theatre,
> The lights are extinguished, for the scene to be changed. (p. 27)

CHAPTER 21

The Living Parent Within You

The relationship with your parent as you had known it in your everyday life ends when the parent dies. However, within you there is an unfolding, ongoing relationship that continues to provide many opportunities for healing. This can be confusing to many who associate death with the termination of a relationship on all levels.

For example, one client shared a dream in which she stood over her father's dead body, concerned about some aspect of preparing his body for burial. Just then, her father, fully alive, walked into the room and, bending over the body, offered some suggestions. The woman became very agitated and confused as she looked from her father's dead body on the floor to the living father talking beside her.

As we explored the dream together, I was struck with the powerful, yet seemingly paradoxical, image of two fathers alive and dead in the same room. The dead one she had learned to accept, for her father had died years before. She had never grieved about his death, quickly putting him out of her mind and immersing herself in teenage activities. Only now in our sessions was she beginning to feel the magnitude of her loss. It was the living father that made her so anxious in the dream: How could he now be appearing so vividly to her, when he had been dead for so many years? She did not know how to relate to him at all. The dream seemed to be suggesting that within her a living father now sought her attention, challenging her to come into a relationship with him while still accepting that he was dead.

While you may have already contacted your parent through previous exercises, you may want to learn ways to continue to contact this living parent within you. You may feel the desire to do this at certain points, perhaps on the anniversary of your parent's death or on his or her birthday. We will explore here two methods for contacting the parent within you: using active imagination and taking a shamanic journey with a clear intention to visit your parent.

Active Imagination:

Close your eyes and imagine a rose that represents your relationship with your parent. Notice its stage of growth—is it tightly closed, beginning to open, blossoming? Enjoy this rose with all your senses—smell it, touch it, look at it.

The rose is now beginning to open slowly, petal by petal. At its center, at the heart of your relationship, stands your parent, waiting for you. Go to meet your parent there, and allow your interaction to unfold on its own. You may be surprised at what happens between you, perhaps some interaction or communication that you never imagined possible in life.

This also may be a time to update your relationship. Share with your parent the changes, feelings, insights, and new perspectives you have experienced in your grief. There may be issues you have recently uncovered that you want to explore with your parent.

When you are ready, conclude your visit. If you still feel unfinished, let him or her know when you will be visiting again. Then step out of the rose's center and watch the petals slowly fold up again, enclosing and protecting the place of your meeting.

A participant in one of my workshops feared that over time the memories of his mother would fade, taking away the last vestiges he held of her. I suggested that working with some active imagination techniques might provide an opportunity to bring the relationship up to the present rather than clinging to past memories.

Although he was doubtful that anything would happen, he closed his eyes and began to visualize a rose opening, according to my instructions. At its center his mother spontaneously appeared, shocking him with the power of her presence. The two of them sat together for a long time, talking and touching. As my client opened his eyes, he sat stunned for a long time, assimilating the impact of the experience. Then he shifted in his chair, smiled, and began to speak about what had happened to him. His mother had felt very real. He had touched her, heard her voice, and seen her vividly. He felt a profound peace knowing that within him his mother was accessible to him, in a different form perhaps than he had known when she was alive but with an even greater power to move him.

Shamanic Journey:

Prepare for the journey as was discussed in Chapter Ten. Then as you begin your journey, define for yourself what you want to accomplish, such as contacting your parent to see how he or she is doing in the spirit world. Black Elk, medicine man of the Oglala Sioux, taught that young willows "have a lesson to teach us, for in the fall their leaves die and return to the earth, but in the spring they come to life again. So, too, men die but live again in the real world of Wakan-Tanka, where there is nothing but the spirit of things" (quoted by Joseph Brown in *The Sacred Pipe*, p. 32).

In shamanic tradition it is very important that a dying person be guided into the next reality. As Michael Harner stresses in his workshops on this subject, without this guidance, it is possible that the person will be lost in transit and unable to complete the transition into the light. As a result, the person's spirit can remain restless and depressed. Sometimes in a sudden or violent death the person's spirit can wander in a daze, without any awareness that death has even occurred. The shaman travels into nonordinary reality to find these spirits, educate them about their situation, and guide them toward the light. So it is possible that your parent is struggling in his or her passage.

As the drumming begins, state clearly to yourself that your intention in your journey is to find your parent's spirit. Ask for help in this task from your guides if you wish. As it may be a long search through many levels of the three worlds, you may not find your parent on the first attempt. Be persistent.

When you find your parent, you may be surprised, reassured, or disturbed by his or her state of being. If your parent seems unhappy, restless, or depressed, he or she may need your support or guidance. Ask what your parent wants, where he or she wants to go. Perhaps there is some healing you can facilitate. If your parent seems disoriented and confused, without any awareness that he or she has died, you may need to share the circumstances of the death or even take your parent to the location where death occurred so that the scene can be relived. Again, some healing may be called for before your parent is ready to settle into the spirit world. Follow your intuition. If you feel confused about what to do next, ask your guide for help.

If there are issues you need to bring up with your parent, take some time to communicate and explore together whatever is unhealed or unfinished, and share what has healed. You may find that your parent sees things in a very different way than in life, thus providing new opportunities for healing.

When the drums signal that it is time to return, bring your visit to some conclusion and find your way back to the tunnel.

As you make contact in this way from time to time, you will notice that the many changes you are undergoing in your grief will be reflected in a changing relationship to your parent. It becomes clear that death has terminated the form of the relationship in one reality, only to reveal another one shimmering like a multifaceted diamond with the promise of new discoveries.

CHAPTER 22

The Dance of the Sun and the Moon

Near the anniversary of my first shamanic journeys, I had a disturbing yet healing journey that initiated a shift in my depression. A year before, the images of my inner journeys had likewise created a change in my approach to Dad's illness.

> *I follow the tunnel to its opening, where Xan is waiting for me. As we enter his cave, I ask Xan for help with my depression (strange as it may seem, it hadn't occurred to me before this to ask for help). My attention is drawn to a large white tube on the ceiling. It begins to move. Apprehensively, I watch as it starts to slide down the cave wall—with a shiver I realize that it is a thick white snake.*
>
> *It winds around my feet, entwining my body with tight, squeezing coils. Like a mummy, I cannot move, and I am terrified. As its head hovers over mine, a stone glowing at its forehead, it suddenly strikes, biting the top of my head hard. It then darts its tongue into the bloody wound, my body lighting up with veins of fiery electricity. The hot fire cuts new pathways in a vast network. I struggle against the pain, but I cannot move at all. As the drums call me back, the snake reluctantly releases its grip.*

As I opened my eyes, the world came flooding in in joyous waves. I laughed as my body pulsed with happiness. The depression had lifted! It was hard for me to comprehend how the snake had changed my state, so I watched myself suspiciously throughout the rest of the evening. The depression did not return.

I awakened the next morning, half expecting to feel that dark cloud hovering over me. Instead, the room was filled with light, the song of birds welcoming me to the new day. As I sat drinking in the magic of the moment, celebrating life with all my senses, an inspiring idea formed in my mind for a new project. The excitement and gratitude that I felt in response summoned a deluge of energy. I bounded from my bed that morning, remembering how often periods of depression and sterility precede a creative breakthrough.

Two weeks before the anniversary of my father's death, illness struck our household. Taylor and then Jon succumbed to a debilitating flu. Dropping all outside obligations in order to take care of them, I withdrew into our home. Then when they had healed, I got sick.

When my power animal carried me in his arms to the dark underworld, saying, "Trust us," I knew that I would not spring out of bed the next day. I understood that my body was now seeking to assimilate the changes of the previous months. As I have seen with so many clients, after a period of intensive growth, the body needs to build a new order that integrates these changes; but it must break down the old order first, often through illness. Days passed as my feverish and aching body lay limply on the bed, surrendered to doing nothing.

I often thought of my father; a year ago he had been confined to his bed, unable to move. Vivid pictures of him in his hospital room along with the images of my journeys during that time floated through my mind. However, unlike in the months before, this was not painful; I felt at peace, full of love for my father. As the days passed, I hovered between the worlds, sensing in my groggy state that many layers in me were healing simultaneously.

As the energy returned to my body, the first blossoms were appearing on the almond tree, and the air was sweet and fresh. My senses gratefully drank in life once again, rejoicing in simple things—moving and stretching my body, feeling the sunlight on my skin, visiting with friends, tasting food.

I was excited to join my friends at our weekly shamanic journey group. That night I had a very moving journey that confirmed the healing that had taken place during my illness.

A young man, radiating purity and innocence, is waiting for me at the end of the tunnel. We run together up a mountain, following a path that circles around it in a spiral fashion. We run with perfect rhythm and concentration, our bodies flowing into each step without tiring.

At the top of the mountain is a blue lake, bordered by shimmering crystals. The young man tells me that we must walk around this lake in the sacred manner. He begins walking slowly, meditatively, with head bowed, and I follow. As we come to the point of each direction, I raise my head to the heavens as I see him do, receiving the full power of that direction. We continue in this way until I reach the north. He stands opposite me in the south.

As our eyes lock, a rainbow arches between us over the lake. Waves of thought forms and colors pass from him to me and from me to him. When a flood of brilliant light passes into me, I feel an intense tingling sensation. Looking down, I see that my body has become a shimmering rainbow body. Then my body falls away and only rainbow light shimmers in the sky. The young man calls me back; I am standing opposite him again, but in the place of the rainbow arch there now hovers a golden egg. The egg vibrates and enters my womb.

We commence walking so that I am in the west and he in the east. Behind him I can see the sun rising; behind me the moon is setting in the night sky. Suddenly I am suspended over the lake, the sun and the moon dancing in my body. The sun appears in my right hand, the moon in my left; my hands dance together. The sun illuminates my head, the moon my womb; then they dance, changing places, and come together in my chest.

As they merge, my whole body lights up, and I drop through the lake, down through dark depths into a large cavern lighted by a hundred candles. Along the walls Native Americans are sitting, intensely absorbed in their drumming. They gesture for me to draw in the sand what I have just experienced above the lake. I kneel down,

drawing a sun with a moon crescent within it. Around this
I walk barefoot, my footprints creating a spiral pattern.

Then I return to sit in the center. My tracks have
transformed into snakes that circle around the drawing of
the sun and the moon. Two green snakes crawl on me,
entering my mouth. I try to clamp my jaw to keep them
out, but one of the Native Americans urges me to let them
in. One goes to my chest and one to my womb, coiling
around the golden egg.

With the dance of the sun and the moon, I could feel a joining
of the male and female energies within me, and with it a new
feeling of balance, strength, and vulnerability. In alchemy the
union of the sun, which represents the masculine principle, and
the moon, which represents the feminine principle, brings the
peace that can be found only when the opposites have come
together.

As the anniversary of my father's death approached, the
imagery of my journeys and dreams hinted at impending
changes. Over years of working with my dreams I have learned
that a shift in inner imagery is often followed by changes in my
life. This signaled to me that the forces that had stirred within for
so many months were now preparing to press outward, a new
beginning tentatively making its way into the outer world. Somehow, in a way I could not define, I felt different. Grief had
hollowed great empty spaces in my being. There was a new
spaciousness through which life flowed without hindrance, so
many experiences, thoughts, and feelings coming and going.
There was room for it all—the hurt, joy, loneliness, and love.
There was room for paradox and mystery, room for surprise.

In preparation for the anniversary of my father's death, I
took a journey:

A majestic woman, her white robe gracefully cascading
into a ring of foaming waves at her feet, leads me up a
spiral stair that entwines around the massive trunk of a
gigantic tree. We climb a long time, rising higher and
higher. As the atmosphere grows progressively thinner and
brighter, my eyes squint and I struggle to fill my lungs

*with air. Finally she stops, pointing to my father, who is
waiting in bright sunlight.*

*Dad is radiant, beaming joyously, with little lights
sparkling all over his head. I am stunned by the change in
him since my last journey, in which he was grieving over
the hurts he had caused in his life.*

*Smiling, he gathers me in his arms in a loving
embrace. "I have healed, thanks to you all. I am very
happy." He looks closely at me, his eyes probing. "You
still harbor a little resentment toward me, don't you?" I
do feel it as he speaks, but in the circle of his love I can
feel it dissolving away. I hug him close, asking him, "Dad,
what do you want me to do on the anniversary of your
death?"*

*He thinks a moment and replies, "Dance, dance with
life and joy. Let life move your body." Moved by this
unexpected request, I ask if there is anything else he
wishes to impart to me. He tells me to enjoy life more,
to stop and savor the little moments. This is indeed a very
different perspective than the driving, achievement-
oriented one he had had in life. As he starts to fade, I feel
no regret or longing for him to stay longer. Our contact
has been very full and loving.*

On the anniversary of Dad's death, I lit a candle before his
picture. The deeply moving chords of Samuel Barber's Adagio
for Strings, Opus 11, filled the room, inviting the first small,
tentative movements. Soon my body, flowing, expanding, con-
tracting, gliding, reaching, surging, arching, had slipped inside
the pulsing heart of the music. Any sense of someone dancing
melted away—the dance was dancing itself. Its exquisite vehicle,
my body, flowed from movement to movement on a swelling tide
of sound, borne by a rhythm that had its own wisdom, the
rhythm of the dance of fields of energy, the pulse of life. Life itself
moved me to dance, my cells vibrating and humming, my arms
reaching to stir the stars—a miracle at every step. I wept and
laughed, as Dad's presence swept through me in tingling waves of
joy. Everything is within reach, everything is alive!

CHAPTER 23

The Music of Life

Grief has its own nature, rhythm, and timing, and these often do not fit into our ideas of experience of grief. The forces behind grief are powerful enough to wreak havoc with our attempts to order and control our world. There is no map to follow, no schedule to adhere to.

So many clients have complained to me, "It's been two months . . . six months . . . a year; why am I still feeling this way? I should be over this by now." Many become impatient in their long passage in the second stage of grief. They feel that it will never end. But the timing cannot be predicted or rushed.

Our journey through grief is a long and arduous passage, requiring much courage and patience. We move through shock; we descend into the darkness for what seems to be an eternity. There we are buffeted by intense emotions, unpredictable and uncontrollable. We watch the familiar supports of our lives undermined, our assumptions shattered. We suffer the agony of loss and loneliness and are tortured with unanswered questions.

The death of a parent wounds us deeply, but if we are willing to descend into the depths of our grief, our wounding becomes a healing. As we retreat to our sanctuary, we withdraw into the womb of our grief, where we can fully mourn our loss, heal our wounds, and contact the deep source of life within. Our sanctuary becomes a place of gestation, preparing us in the darkness for an emergence into a larger world that will come naturally in its own time, as naturally as birth. If we can let grief guide us through chaos and suffering, if we can trust grief as it shatters old visions and structures, then our loss can become an initiation into greater life.

Then one day the dark passage opens, revealing a new landscape. Eyes revel in brilliant color, hearts throb with love. We have emerged into a new life and see through new eyes. As Siddhartha, in Hermann Hesse's book, discovered on the banks of the river, "The laughter of the wise, the cry of the indignant, and the groan of the dying. They were all interwoven and interlocked, entwined in a thousand ways . . . all of them together with the world, all of them together with the stream of events and the music of life" (p. 135).

Then we realize how much more there is to life and that we have been living only a small and limited portion of all the possibilities inherent within this magnificent and mysterious universe. As we emerge from the dark passage, we are propelled into "the stream of events and the music of life," eager to live more fully on this earth.

Nature calls to us to rejoice in her beauty, to revel in her life force stirring everywhere. The cycle of her days and her seasons restores us to the natural procession of our own inner cycles of death and rebirth, of flowering and fading, of withdrawal and emergence. We learn to allow the seasons to move unhindered through our lives. Each moment becomes precious, an opportunity to embrace the wonder of life—the hopes, the joys, the pain, the ecstasy, the separations, the losses, the meetings, the conflicts, the peace.

We emerge ready to experience not only a fuller, larger life than we had known on this earth but also an invisible one that coexists with our daily habitat. The wounds of our grief become the passports into this world that we perceive with our imagination. The door is open for us to cross over—if we do not go back to sleep and fall into the old constricting patterns. The Sufi poet Rumi urges us in *Open Secret,* "People are going back and forth across the doorsill where the two worlds touch. The door is round and open. Don't go back to sleep" (p. 7).

Bibliography

Achterberg, Jeanne. *Imagery in Healing: Shamanism and Modern Medicine*. Boston: Shambhala, 1985.

Avens, Roberts. *Imagination Is Reality*. Dallas, TX: Spring Publications, 1980.

Bennett, Hal Zina. *Inner Guides, Visions, Dreams and Dr. Einstein*. Berkeley, CA: Celestial Arts, 1986.

Berry, Patricia. "An Approach to the Dream," *Spring* (1974):58–79.

Bloomfield, Harold. *Making Peace With Your Parents*. New York: Ballantine Press, 1983.

Bly, Robert. *The Kabir Book: Forty-Four of the Ecstatic Poems of Kabir*. Boston: Beacon Press, 1971.

Borysenko, Joan. *Guilt Is the Teacher, Love Is the Lesson*. New York: Warner Books, 1990.

Bradshaw, John. *Bradshaw on: The Family*. Deerfield Beach, FL: Health Communications, 1988.

Bragdon, Emma. *The Call of Spiritual Emergency*. San Francisco: Harper & Row, 1990.

Brown, Joseph Epes. *The Sacred Pipe: Black Elk's Account of the Seven Rites of the Oglala Sioux*. New York: Penguin Books, 1953.

de Chardin, Teilhard. *The Phenomenon of Man*. New York: Harper & Row, 1959.

Doore, Gary. *Shaman's Path*. Boston: Shambhala, 1988.

Eliade, Mircea. *Shamanism*. Translated by Wilard R. Trask. New York: Bollingen Foundation, 1964.

———. *Rites and Symbols of Initiation*. New York: Harper Torchbooks, 1958.

Eliot, T. S. *Four Quartets*. New York: Harcourt Brace Jovanovich, 1943.

Freemantle, Francesca, and Chogyam Trungpa., trans. *The Tibetan Book of the Dead*. Boulder, CO: Shambhala, 1975.

Goldstein, Joseph. *The Experience of Insight: A Natural Unfolding*. Santa Cruz, CA: Unity Press, 1976.

Grof, Stanislav, and Christina Grof. *Spiritual Emergency*. Los Angeles: Tarcher, 1989.

———. *The Stormy Search for the Self: Understanding and Coping with Spiritual Emergency*. Los Angeles: Tarcher, 1990.

Grosso, Michael. *The Final Choice*. Walpole, NH: Stillpoint, 1985.

Halifax, Joan. *Shamanic Voices*. New York: Dutton, 1979.

Hannah, Barbara. *Active Imagination*. Boston: Sigo Press, 1981.

Harner, Michael. *The Way of the Shaman*. San Francisco: Harper & Row, 1980 and 1990.

Hesse, Hermann. *Siddhartha*. New York: Bantam, 1951.

Hillman, James. *Re-Visioning Psychology*. New York: Harper & Row, 1975.

———. *The Dream and the Underworld*. New York: Harper & Row, 1979.

Hine, Virginia. *Last Letter to the Pebble People*. Santa Cruz, CA: Unity Press, 1977.

Horn, Frances. *I Want One Thing*. Marina del Rey, CA: DeVorss & Co., 1981.

Houston, Jean. *The Search for the Beloved*. Los Angeles: Tarcher, 1987.

Howell, Alice. *The Dove in the Stone: Finding the Sacred in the Commonplace*. Wheaton, IL: Theosophical Publishing House, 1988.

Johnson, Robert A. *Inner Work*. San Francisco: Harper & Row, 1986.

Jung, C. G. *The Collected Works of C. G. Jung*. 20 vols. Translated by R. F. C. Hull. Bollingen Series XX. Princeton, NJ: Princeton University Press, 1957–79.

———. *Dream Analysis*. Princeton, NJ: Princeton University Press, 1984.

———. *Dreams*. Princeton, NJ: Princeton University Press, 1974.

Kalweit, Holger. *Dreamtime and Inner Space*. Boston: Shambhala, 1988.

Kazantzakis, Nikos. *Saint Francis*. New York: Simon and Schuster, 1962.

Kinney, Jay. "The Gnosis Interview: June Singer." *Gnosis*, (Winter 1989): 16–21.

Kornfield, Jack, and Paul Breiter. *A Still Forest Pool: The Insight Meditation of Achaan Chah*. Wheaton, IL: Theosophical Publishing House, 1985.

Kübler-Ross, Elisabeth. *On Death and Dying*. New York: Knopf, 1981.

———. *Death: The Final Stage of Growth*. Englewood Cliffs, NJ: Prentice-Hall, 1975.

Levine, Stephen. *Healing Into Life and Death*. Garden City, NY: Anchor Press, 1987.

———. *Meetings at the Edge*. Garden City, NY: Anchor Press, 1984.

———. *Who Dies?* Garden City, NY: Anchor Press, 1982.

Mindell, Arnold. *Working with the Dreaming Body*. Boston: Routledge and Kegan Paul, 1985.

———. *Coma*. Boston: Shambhala, 1989.

Moody, Raymond, Jr. *Life After Life*. New York: Bantam Books, 1975.

Moustakas, Clark E. *Loneliness*. Englewood Cliffs, NJ: Spectrum Books, 1961.

———. *Loneliness and Love*. Englewood Cliffs, NJ: Spectrum Books, 1972.

Moyers, Bill, and Robert Bly. *A Gathering of Men*. Cooper Station, NY: Mystic Fire Video, 1990. Video.

Myers, Edward. *When Parents Die: A Guide for Adults.* New York: Viking, 1986.

Neumann, Erich. *The Origins and History of Consciousness.* Princeton, NJ: Princeton University Press, 1954.

Progoff, Ira. *At a Journal Workshop.* New York: Dialogue House Library, 1975.

Rilke, Rainer Maria. *Letters to a Young Poet.* Translated by M. D. Herter Norton. New York: Norton, 1934.

Ring, Kenneth. *Heading Toward Omega.* New York: Morrow, 1984.

Rumi, Jelaluddin. *The Ruins of the Heart.* Translated by Edmund Helminski. Putney, VT: Threshold Books, 1987.

———. *Open Secret: Versions of Rumi.* Translated by John Moyne and Coleman Barks. Putney, VT: Threshold Books, 1984.

Russell, George William. *The Candle of Vision.* Wheaton, IL: Theosophical Publishing House, 1974.

Sanford, John A. *Dreams and Healing.* New York: Paulist Press, 1978.

Singer, June. *Seeing Through the Invisible World.* San Francisco: Harper & Row, 1990.

Tatelbaum, Judy. *The Courage to Grieve.* New York: Harper & Row, 1980.

Van Dusen, Wilson. *The Natural Depth in Man.* New York: Harper & Row, 1972.

Von Franz, Marie-Louise. *On Dreams and Death.* Boston: Shambhala, 1987.

Walsh, Roger. *The Spirit of Shamanism.* Los Angeles: Tarcher, 1990.

Watkins, Mary. *Waking Dreams.* Dallas, TX: Spring Publications, 1976.

Whitmont, Edward. *The Symbolic Quest.* Princeton, NJ: Princeton University Press, 1969.

Index